MW01439541

Building an Offensive Security Lab for Enterprise Cyber Teams

Building an Offensive Security Lab for Enterprise Cyber Teams 1
Introduction 4
Chapter 1: Introduction to Offensive Security 6
Chapter 2: Understanding the Threat Landscape 8
Chapter 3: Key Components of an Offensive Security Lab 11
Chapter 4: Selecting the Right Tools and Technologies 14
Chapter 5: Designing a Scalable Lab Infrastructure 20
Chapter 6: Setting Up a Virtualized Environment 25
Chapter 7: Deploying Network Architectures 31
Configuring Routing and Switching 32
Chapter 8: Integrating Threat Intelligence Platforms 36
Chapter 9: Simulating Advanced Persistent Threats (APTs) 42

Chapter 10: Developing Custom Exploits and Payloads 48

Developing Custom Payloads 50

Chapter 11: Red Team Operations: Strategies and Tactics 54

Understanding Red Team Operations.. 54

Planning Red Team Operations 55

Develop a Threat Model 55

Select Tactics, Techniques, and Procedures (TTPs) 56

Establish Rules of Engagement 56

Assemble the Red Team 57

Executing Red Team Operations 57

Exit and Cleanup 58

Chapter 12: Monitoring and Logging for Offensive Labs 61

The Importance of Monitoring and Logging 61

Key Components of Monitoring and Logging 61

Log Collection and Aggregation... 62

Real-Time Monitoring 62

Alerting and Notifications 63

Log Storage and Retention 63

Correlation and Analysis 64

Implementing Monitoring and Logging in Your Offensive Lab 64

Perform Post-Incident Analysis 66

Update Security Measures... 66

Enhance Threat Detection and Response 67

Regularly Review and Refine Monitoring Strategies 67

Chapter 13: Conducting Security Assessments and Penetration Tests 69

The Purpose of Security Assessments and Penetration Tests 69

Planning and Scoping Security Assessments and Penetration Tests 70

Define Objectives.. 70

Determine Scope 70

Establish Rules of Engagement 71
Select the Testing Methodology 71
Conduct Risk Assessments 72
Reconnaissance and Information Gathering 73
Vulnerability Scanning 73
Post-Exploitation 74
Chapter 14: Training and Skill Development for Cyber Teams 76
The Importance of Hands-On Training 76
Developing a Training Program 77
Set Training Objectives 78
Design Training Scenarios 78
Implement Blended Learning 79
Encourage Continuous Learning 79
Chapter 15: Maintaining and Evolving the Security Lab 82
The Importance of Continuous Maintenance 83
Routine Maintenance Activities 83
Hardware Maintenance 84
Backup and Disaster Recovery 84
Network and Security Configurations 84
Documentation and Inventory Management 85
Evolving the Lab to Meet New Challenges 85
Expand Testing Capabilities 85
Integrate Emerging Technologies 86
Simulate Advanced Threats 86
Plan for Future Growth 87
Stay Informed and Adapt 87
Leveraging the Lab as a Strategic Asset 88
Enhance Security Testing and Assurance 88
Support Incident Response and Threat Hunting 88

Facilitate Research and Development 88

Provide Training and Skill Development 89

Contribute to Organizational Resilience 89

Conclusion 89

Introduction

In today's digital age, where cyber threats have become increasingly sophisticated, the need for robust cybersecurity practices has never been more crucial. As enterprises strive to protect their digital assets, they often find themselves in a reactive stance, responding to breaches and attacks after the fact. However, a shift toward a proactive security approach is not just necessary but essential. This is where offensive security comes into play.

Offensive security is the practice of simulating cyber attacks to identify and mitigate vulnerabilities before malicious actors can exploit them. It involves understanding the mindset of a hacker, anticipating their moves, and fortifying defenses accordingly. But to do this effectively, organizations need a controlled environment where they can safely test their systems and train their security teams. This environment is known as an offensive security lab.

Building an Offensive Security Lab for Enterprise Cyber Teams is a comprehensive guide designed to help organizations create a powerful, scalable, and flexible lab environment that supports advanced cybersecurity operations. Whether you're a seasoned security professional or a newcomer looking to bolster your organization's defenses, this book will walk you through the process of building an offensive security lab from the ground up.

The importance of an offensive security lab cannot be overstated. It serves as a sandbox where security teams can simulate real-world attacks, test new tools, and refine their tactics without risking the integrity of live systems. In this lab, red teams can engage in mock cyber battles, exploring vulnerabilities in a controlled manner and developing strategies to defend against them. Moreover, it provides a platform for continuous learning, enabling cyber teams to stay ahead of emerging threats.

This book begins with an introduction to offensive security, laying the foundation for why such an approach is vital in today's threat landscape. We explore the various types of threats that organizations face, from common malware to sophisticated advanced persistent threats (APTs), and discuss how an offensive mindset can turn the tide in the ongoing battle against cyber adversaries.

The subsequent chapters delve into the specifics of lab construction, starting with the key components necessary for an effective offensive security lab. From hardware and software considerations to network configurations and virtualization options, we cover every aspect of building a robust infrastructure that can scale with your organization's needs.

One of the critical decisions in setting up a lab is selecting the right tools and technologies. With a vast array of security tools available on the market, choosing the ones that align with your objectives can be daunting. This book provides guidance on evaluating and selecting tools that complement your lab's goals, ensuring that you have the necessary capabilities to simulate attacks, analyze vulnerabilities, and defend against them.

Designing a scalable lab infrastructure is another crucial step. As your organization grows, so too will the demands on your security lab. We'll discuss best practices for building a flexible infrastructure that can accommodate increased workloads and integrate seamlessly with your existing IT environment.

The book also emphasizes the importance of integrating threat intelligence into your lab. Threat intelligence platforms offer insights into the latest tactics, techniques, and procedures (TTPs) used by cyber adversaries. By incorporating these insights into your lab environment, you can simulate realistic attack scenarios and prepare your team to respond effectively.

As we progress through the chapters, we explore advanced topics such as simulating APTs, developing custom exploits, and conducting red team operations. These sections are designed to challenge even the most experienced security professionals, pushing them to hone their skills and think creatively about defense strategies.

Finally, the book addresses the ongoing need for training and skill development. The cyber threat landscape is constantly evolving, and so too must your team's abilities. We discuss methods for using your offensive security lab as a training ground, helping your cyber teams stay sharp and ready to tackle the next wave of threats.

Building an Offensive Security Lab for Enterprise Cyber Teams is more than just a technical manual—it's a strategic guide for empowering your organization to take control of its cybersecurity destiny. By investing in an offensive security lab, you're not just preparing for the next attack; you're taking a proactive stance in the war against cyber threats, turning the tables on adversaries and securing your digital future.

Chapter 1: Introduction to Offensive Security

Offensive security is a paradigm shift in the way organizations approach cybersecurity. Traditionally, cybersecurity has been largely defensive in nature, focusing on building barriers and responding to attacks as they occur. Firewalls, antivirus software, and intrusion detection systems are all examples of defensive measures designed to keep attackers out. However, as cyber threats have grown more sophisticated, it has become clear that defensive measures alone are not enough. Enter offensive security.

Offensive security is about taking the fight to the adversary. It involves actively seeking out vulnerabilities in your systems, exploiting them in a controlled environment, and then patching them before a real attacker can do so. This proactive approach is designed to uncover weaknesses that may not be apparent through defensive monitoring alone. By thinking like a hacker, organizations can better anticipate and mitigate potential attacks.

The concept of offensive security is not entirely new. It has its roots in military strategy, where the idea of "know your enemy" has long been a guiding principle. In the context of cybersecurity, this means understanding the tactics, techniques, and procedures (TTPs) used by attackers, and then using that knowledge to strengthen your own defenses. Offensive security teams, often referred to as red teams, simulate cyber attacks on their own organizations to test the effectiveness of their security measures.

One of the key benefits of offensive security is that it allows organizations to identify and fix vulnerabilities before they can be exploited by malicious actors. This is particularly important given the increasing complexity of modern IT environments. With the proliferation of cloud computing, mobile devices, and Internet of Things (IoT) devices, the attack surface for organizations has expanded dramatically. Each of these technologies introduces new vulnerabilities that can be exploited by attackers, and it is often difficult for traditional defensive measures to keep up.

Offensive security also plays a critical role in incident response. By regularly testing their systems through simulated attacks, organizations can better prepare for real-world incidents. This includes not only identifying vulnerabilities but also developing and refining incident response procedures. When a real attack occurs, the organization is better equipped to respond quickly and effectively, minimizing damage and reducing downtime.

Another important aspect of offensive security is the use of threat intelligence. Threat intelligence involves collecting and analyzing data on the latest cyber threats, including the TTPs used by attackers. This information is then used to inform offensive security operations, allowing organizations to simulate realistic attack scenarios. By staying up-to-date on the latest threats, organizations can ensure that their security measures are effective against the most current threats.

Building an offensive security lab is the first step in implementing an offensive security program. A security lab is a controlled environment where organizations can safely simulate attacks, test new tools, and train their security teams. It serves as a sandbox where red teams can practice their skills and experiment with different attack techniques. By creating a realistic and flexible lab environment, organizations can better prepare for the challenges of the modern threat landscape.

The offensive security lab is not just a tool for red teams; it is a valuable resource for the entire security team. Blue teams, responsible for defending the organization, can use the lab to test their defenses and develop new strategies. Incident response teams can use the lab to practice their procedures and refine their workflows. Even executives can benefit from the lab, gaining a better understanding of the organization's security posture and the potential risks it faces.

In summary, offensive security is a proactive approach to cybersecurity that focuses on identifying and mitigating vulnerabilities before they can be exploited by attackers. By simulating attacks in a controlled environment, organizations can better prepare for real-world incidents and improve their overall security posture. The offensive security lab is a critical component of this approach, providing a safe and flexible environment for testing and training. As cyber threats continue to evolve, offensive security will play an increasingly important role in protecting organizations from harm.

Chapter 2: Understanding the Threat Landscape

Understanding the threat landscape is a critical component of any effective cybersecurity strategy. The threat landscape refers to the ever-changing environment in which cyber threats emerge, evolve, and impact organizations. It encompasses the various types of threats, the motivations behind them, the tactics used by attackers, and the vulnerabilities they exploit. In this chapter, we will explore the key elements of the threat landscape and discuss how organizations can stay informed and prepared to defend against emerging threats.

The threat landscape is dynamic and constantly evolving. New threats are discovered every day, and attackers are continuously developing new tactics to bypass security measures. This makes it challenging for organizations to keep up with the latest developments and protect their systems effectively. However, by understanding the threat landscape, organizations can better anticipate potential attacks and take proactive measures to defend against them.

One of the most common types of cyber threats is malware. Malware is malicious software that is designed to damage or disrupt computer systems. It can take many forms, including viruses, worms, Trojans, and ransomware. Each type of malware has its own characteristics and methods of infection, but the goal is always the same: to compromise the target system. Malware can be delivered through a variety of vectors, such as email attachments, infected websites, or removable media. Once installed on a system, malware can steal sensitive data, disrupt operations, or even render systems unusable.

Another significant threat in the landscape is phishing. Phishing is a social engineering attack that tricks individuals into providing sensitive information, such as login credentials or financial details. Attackers often use email or instant messaging to deliver phishing messages, which appear to be from legitimate sources. These messages typically contain a link to a fake website that closely resembles the real one, where victims are prompted to enter their information. Phishing attacks are highly effective because they exploit human psychology, making them difficult to defend against using technical measures alone.

Advanced Persistent Threats (APTs) represent a more sophisticated class of threats. APTs are long-term, targeted attacks conducted by well-funded and highly skilled adversaries, often nation-states or organized crime groups. Unlike traditional cyber attacks, which may be quick and opportunistic, APTs are methodical and persistent, with attackers maintaining access to a network for extended periods of time. The goal of an APT is typically to steal sensitive data, such as intellectual property or classified information, rather than causing immediate damage. Defending against APTs requires a deep understanding of the attack methods used and a proactive approach to security.

Ransomware has become one of the most disruptive threats in recent years. Ransomware is a type of malware that encrypts the victim's files, rendering them inaccessible until a ransom is paid. Attackers often demand payment in cryptocurrency, making it difficult to trace the funds. Ransomware attacks can have devastating consequences for organizations, leading to significant financial losses and operational disruptions. In some cases, victims have been forced to shut down operations entirely while they attempt to recover from an attack. The rise of ransomware-as-a-service (RaaS) has further exacerbated the threat, enabling even low-skilled attackers to launch sophisticated ransomware attacks.

Insider threats are another critical component of the threat landscape. An insider threat occurs when an individual within an organization, such as an employee or contractor, intentionally or unintentionally compromises security. Insiders may have access to sensitive information, making them a valuable target for attackers. They may also be motivated by a variety of factors, including financial gain, revenge, or coercion. Insider threats are particularly challenging to detect and mitigate because they involve trusted individuals who have legitimate access to the organization's systems and data.

In addition to these specific types of threats, organizations must also contend with vulnerabilities in their systems and software. Vulnerabilities are weaknesses or flaws in software code or hardware design that can be exploited by attackers to gain unauthorized access to a system. Vulnerabilities can exist in operating systems, applications, network devices, and even physical infrastructure. Keeping systems patched and up-to-date is one of the most effective ways to mitigate the risk of exploitation, but this can be challenging in large, complex environments where downtime is not an option.

Staying informed about the threat landscape requires ongoing monitoring and analysis. Threat intelligence is a valuable resource for organizations, providing timely and relevant information about emerging threats, attack methods, and vulnerabilities. Threat intelligence can be gathered from a variety of sources, including security vendors, government agencies, and open-source communities. By integrating threat intelligence into their security operations, organizations can gain a better understanding of the risks they face and take proactive measures to defend against them.

In conclusion, understanding the threat landscape is essential for any organization that wants to protect itself from cyber attacks. The threat landscape is constantly changing, with new threats emerging and existing threats evolving. By staying informed about the latest developments and understanding the tactics used by attackers, organizations can better anticipate and defend against potential attacks. Threat intelligence, proactive security measures, and a deep understanding of the threat landscape are all critical components of a successful cybersecurity strategy.

Chapter 3: Key Components of an Offensive Security Lab

An offensive security lab is a controlled environment designed for testing and refining cybersecurity practices. It is a critical resource for organizations that want to take a proactive approach to security, enabling them to simulate real-world attacks, identify vulnerabilities, and develop effective defense strategies. In this chapter, we will explore the key components of an offensive security lab, including the hardware, software, and network infrastructure needed to create a robust and scalable lab environment.

The first step in building an offensive security lab is selecting the appropriate hardware. The hardware requirements for a security lab can vary depending on the size and scope of the lab, as well as the specific goals of the organization. At a minimum, the lab will need servers, workstations, and networking equipment. Servers are used to host virtual machines (VMs), which simulate the target environment. Workstations are used by security analysts to interact with the lab environment, while networking equipment is used to create the network topologies needed for testing.

One of the most important considerations when selecting hardware is scalability. As the organization's needs grow, the lab must be able to accommodate additional resources and support more complex testing scenarios. This means choosing hardware that can be easily expanded, such as servers with additional RAM and storage capacity, and networking equipment with sufficient ports and throughput to handle increased traffic. Additionally, the hardware should be compatible with the virtualization platforms and other software tools used in the lab.

Virtualization is a key component of any offensive security lab. Virtualization allows multiple VMs to run on a single physical server, enabling the lab to simulate complex environments without the need for a large number of physical machines. VMs can be easily created, modified, and deleted, making them ideal for testing different configurations and attack scenarios. Virtualization platforms, such as VMware vSphere, Microsoft Hyper-V, and open-source options like KVM, provide the tools needed to manage VMs and create network topologies within the lab environment.

In addition to virtualization, the lab will require a variety of software tools for conducting offensive security operations. These tools include vulnerability scanners, penetration testing frameworks, exploit development environments, and forensic analysis tools. Some of the most popular tools used in offensive security labs include:

Nmap: A network scanning tool used to discover hosts and services on a network.

Metasploit: A penetration testing framework that provides a wide range of exploits and payloads for testing vulnerabilities.

Burp Suite: A web vulnerability scanner used to identify security flaws in web applications.

Wireshark: A network protocol analyzer used to capture and analyze network traffic.

Cobalt Strike: A tool for simulating advanced persistent threats and conducting red team operations.

These tools, along with others, form the backbone of the offensive security lab, enabling security teams to simulate attacks, identify vulnerabilities, and develop defense strategies.

Network infrastructure is another critical component of the lab. The network must be designed to replicate the target environment as closely as possible, including the use of firewalls, routers, switches, and other networking devices. The network topology should be flexible, allowing for the creation of different scenarios, such as isolated networks, segmented networks, and fully connected networks. This flexibility is essential for testing different attack vectors and understanding how they impact the overall security posture of the organization.

In addition to the physical network infrastructure, the lab should also include a variety of virtual network configurations. Virtual networks can be created using virtualization platforms or network simulation tools, such as GNS3 or Cisco VIRL. These virtual networks allow for the testing of complex scenarios, such as multi-tiered applications, DMZs (demilitarized zones), and cloud environments, without the need for additional physical hardware.

Another important aspect of the lab is the integration of threat intelligence. Threat intelligence provides insights into the latest tactics, techniques, and procedures (TTPs) used by cyber adversaries. By incorporating threat intelligence into the lab environment, organizations can simulate realistic attack scenarios and develop strategies to defend against them. This may involve creating custom attack scripts based on the TTPs of specific threat actors or using threat intelligence platforms to feed data into the lab environment for real-time analysis.

Finally, the lab should include a robust monitoring and logging infrastructure. Monitoring tools, such as SIEM (Security Information and Event Management) systems, are used to collect and analyze data from the lab environment. This data provides valuable insights into the effectiveness of security measures and helps identify areas for improvement. Logging tools are also essential, as they record all activities within the lab, providing a detailed audit trail for analysis and reporting.

In conclusion, building an offensive security lab requires careful planning and consideration of several key components. The hardware, software, network infrastructure, and monitoring tools must all be carefully selected and configured to create a robust and scalable lab environment. By investing in an offensive security lab, organizations can take a proactive approach to cybersecurity, identifying and mitigating vulnerabilities before they can be exploited by attackers. This not only improves the organization's security posture but also provides a valuable resource for training and skill development.

Chapter 4: Selecting the Right Tools and Technologies

In the journey to build a powerful and effective offensive security lab, selecting the right tools and technologies is a pivotal step. The tools and technologies chosen will not only dictate the lab's capabilities but also shape the overall approach to offensive security within the organization. In this chapter, we will explore the criteria for selecting tools, examine some of the most widely-used technologies in the field, and discuss how to integrate them into your offensive security lab to create a comprehensive and flexible environment.

Understanding the Criteria for Tool Selection

Before diving into specific tools and technologies, it's important to establish the criteria for selecting them. The tools chosen for an offensive security lab should align with the organization's specific goals, budget, and the skill level of the team. Here are some key factors to consider:

Purpose and Use Cases: What specific offensive security tasks do you need the tool to perform? Different tools specialize in different areas—vulnerability scanning, penetration testing, exploit development, network analysis, etc. Ensure that the tools you select cover the full spectrum of your needs.

Scalability and Flexibility: Can the tool scale with your organization's needs? A good tool should be able to handle growing workloads and adapt to different environments, whether it's a small lab setup or a large enterprise network.

Ease of Use and Learning Curve: How easy is the tool to use? Consider the skill level of your team. Some tools, while powerful, may have a steep learning curve and require significant training. Others are more user-friendly but might lack advanced features.

Community Support and Documentation: Tools with strong community support and comprehensive documentation are generally easier to troubleshoot and integrate. An active user community can also provide valuable insights, tutorials, and updates.

Integration with Other Tools: Does the tool integrate well with other tools in your lab environment? Seamless integration can enhance workflows and make it easier to correlate data from different sources.

Cost and Licensing: Budget constraints are always a consideration. Some tools are open-source and free, while others require paid licenses. It's important to balance cost with functionality, ensuring that you get the best value for your investment.

Essential Tools for an Offensive Security Lab

Now, let's delve into some of the essential tools and technologies that should be considered when building your offensive security lab. These tools cover a wide range of functionalities, from network scanning to exploit development, and each plays a critical role in the overall security testing process.

Nmap (Network Mapper)

Nmap is one of the most widely used tools in the security community for network discovery and security auditing. It is used to scan networks and identify hosts, services, and open ports. Nmap provides a variety of scanning techniques, such as SYN scan, UDP scan, and OS detection, making it an invaluable tool for understanding the network landscape before launching more targeted attacks.

Metasploit Framework

The Metasploit Framework is a powerful penetration testing tool that provides a comprehensive suite of exploits, payloads, and auxiliary modules. It allows security professionals to simulate real-world attacks, test vulnerabilities, and develop new exploits. Metasploit's modular architecture and extensive library make it a cornerstone of any offensive security lab.

Burp Suite

Burp Suite is a web vulnerability scanner and security testing tool that is essential for identifying weaknesses in web applications. It includes features like a proxy for intercepting and modifying web traffic, a scanner for automated testing, and various manual testing tools. Burp Suite is particularly useful for testing web applications against OWASP Top 10 vulnerabilities.

Wireshark

Wireshark is a network protocol analyzer that captures and inspects data packets in real-time. It is an indispensable tool for understanding network traffic, diagnosing network issues, and analyzing the behavior of various protocols. Wireshark's ability to dissect a wide range of protocols makes it an essential tool for network analysis and forensic investigations.

Cobalt Strike

Cobalt Strike is a commercial tool that is widely used in red teaming and advanced threat emulation. It allows security teams to simulate advanced persistent threats (APTs) and conduct targeted attacks against enterprise networks. Cobalt Strike includes features like beaconing, command and control (C2) infrastructure, and post-exploitation tools, making it a versatile tool for simulating sophisticated attacks.

John the Ripper

John the Ripper is a fast password cracking tool that supports various password hashes, including those used by UNIX, Windows, and macOS systems. It is often used to test the strength of passwords within an organization and to recover lost passwords. Its ability to crack passwords using dictionary attacks, brute force, and customized rules makes it a powerful addition to the offensive security toolkit.

OWASP ZAP (Zed Attack Proxy)

OWASP ZAP is an open-source web application security scanner that is used to find vulnerabilities in web applications. It is similar to Burp Suite but is freely available and widely used in the security community. ZAP is particularly useful for identifying issues like SQL injection, cross-site scripting (XSS), and other common web vulnerabilities.

Kali Linux

Kali Linux is a Linux distribution specifically designed for penetration testing and offensive security. It comes pre-installed with hundreds of security tools, including Nmap, Metasploit, Wireshark, and John the Ripper. Kali Linux serves as the foundation of many offensive security labs due to its comprehensive toolset and ease of use.

BloodHound

BloodHound is a tool used to analyze Active Directory (AD) environments and identify potential attack paths. It uses graph theory to map out relationships between users, groups, and computers within an AD domain, helping security teams to identify high-value targets and plan their attack strategies.

Mimikatz

Mimikatz is a tool used for post-exploitation activities, particularly for extracting plaintext passwords, hashes, and Kerberos tickets from memory. It is often used in red teaming exercises to demonstrate the risks associated with weak credentials and improper credential management.

Integrating Tools into the Lab Environment

Once the tools have been selected, the next step is to integrate them into your lab environment. This involves setting up the tools on your lab's infrastructure, configuring them to work together, and establishing workflows that mimic real-world attack scenarios.

Tool Installation and Configuration

Begin by installing the tools on the appropriate servers or workstations within your lab environment. For instance, Metasploit and Nmap might be installed on dedicated penetration testing servers, while Burp Suite and OWASP ZAP are installed on machines used for web application testing. Ensure that each tool is properly configured according to the specific needs of your testing environment.

Network Configuration

Your lab's network should be configured to allow the tools to interact with each other and with the target systems. For example, you may need to configure firewalls to allow traffic from your scanning tools to the target network or set up VPNs to simulate remote attacks. Network segmentation can be used to create isolated environments for different types of tests, ensuring that tools do not interfere with each other.

Automation and Scripting

Automation can greatly enhance the efficiency of your lab operations. Consider using scripting languages like Python or Bash to automate repetitive tasks, such as scanning, exploitation, and reporting. Tools like Metasploit and Nmap have built-in scripting capabilities that allow you to automate complex attack chains.

Integrating Threat Intelligence

Incorporate threat intelligence into your lab environment to simulate current and emerging threats. For example, you can use threat intelligence feeds to create custom attack scenarios that mimic the tactics of known adversaries. This will help your team practice responding to the latest threats and develop strategies to mitigate them.

Testing and Validation

Once the tools are integrated, conduct a series of tests to validate the lab environment. This might include running vulnerability scans against known targets, executing penetration tests, or simulating phishing attacks. The goal is to ensure that the tools are functioning as expected and that the lab environment accurately reflects real-world conditions.

Continuous Monitoring and Improvement

Offensive security is not a one-time exercise; it requires continuous monitoring and improvement. Regularly update your tools and technologies to ensure they remain effective against new threats. Additionally, review and refine your lab's configurations and workflows based on the results of your testing exercises.

Conclusion

Selecting the right tools and technologies is critical to the success of your offensive security lab. The tools you choose should align with your organization's goals, be scalable and flexible, and integrate well with other components of your lab environment. By carefully selecting and integrating these tools, you can create a powerful lab environment that enables your team to simulate real-world attacks, identify vulnerabilities, and develop effective defense strategies.

In the next chapter, we will explore how to design a scalable lab infrastructure that can grow with your organization's needs, ensuring that your lab remains a valuable resource for years to come.

Chapter 5: Designing a Scalable Lab Infrastructure

Designing a scalable lab infrastructure is a crucial step in building an effective offensive security lab. A well-designed infrastructure ensures that your lab can handle increasing workloads, support more complex testing scenarios, and accommodate the growing needs of your organization. In this chapter, we will discuss the key considerations for designing a scalable lab infrastructure, including hardware selection, network design, and virtualization strategies.

Understanding Scalability

Scalability refers to the ability of your lab infrastructure to grow and adapt as your needs change. A scalable lab can support a larger number of virtual machines (VMs), handle more traffic, and integrate new tools and technologies without significant reconfiguration. Scalability is particularly important for offensive security labs because the complexity and scope of testing scenarios can vary widely, from simple vulnerability scans to full-scale red team operations.

Hardware Selection for Scalability

The foundation of any scalable lab infrastructure is the hardware. When selecting hardware, it's important to consider both the immediate needs of your lab and its potential growth over time. Here are some key factors to consider:

Processing Power

The central processing unit (CPU) is one of the most critical components of your lab's hardware. Offensive security operations, such as vulnerability scanning, exploitation, and network simulation, can be CPU-intensive. Choose servers with multi-core processors that can handle multiple VMs and processes simultaneously. Additionally, consider using servers with virtualization-specific CPUs that are optimized for running virtual environments.

Memory (RAM)

Memory is another crucial factor in determining the scalability of your lab. Each VM in your lab environment requires a certain amount of RAM to function effectively. As the number of VMs increases, so does the demand for memory. To ensure scalability, choose servers with high memory capacity and the ability to expand memory as needed. Consider using dynamic memory allocation features available in virtualization platforms to optimize memory usage across VMs.

Storage

Storage requirements for an offensive security lab can be significant, especially when dealing with large datasets, logs, and VM snapshots. Choose storage solutions that offer high capacity, fast read/write speeds, and redundancy. Consider using a combination of solid-state drives (SSDs) for fast access and traditional hard disk drives (HDDs) for bulk storage. Additionally, storage area networks (SANs) or network-attached storage (NAS) devices can provide scalable and centralized storage options for your lab.

Networking Equipment

Networking equipment is essential for creating the network topologies needed for testing. Choose routers, switches, and firewalls that offer high throughput, multiple ports, and support for advanced networking features such as VLANs, VPNs, and QoS (Quality of Service). Scalable networking equipment allows you to segment networks, simulate different environments, and manage traffic effectively as your lab grows.

Network Design for Scalability

A scalable network design is crucial for supporting complex and varied testing scenarios. Here are some key considerations for designing a scalable network infrastructure:

Network Segmentation

Network segmentation involves dividing your lab's network into smaller, isolated segments, each with its own set of security controls. Segmentation allows you to simulate different network environments, such as internal corporate networks, DMZs (demilitarized zones), and cloud environments. It also helps contain any potential security breaches within specific segments, preventing them from affecting the entire lab.

Virtual Networks

Virtual networks are an essential component of a scalable lab infrastructure. Virtual networks can be created using network virtualization platforms or hypervisor-based networking features. These networks allow you to simulate complex topologies without the need for additional physical hardware. Virtual networks are also highly flexible, enabling you to reconfigure them quickly to meet different testing needs.

Bandwidth Management

As the number of VMs and the complexity of testing scenarios increase, so does the demand for network bandwidth. Ensure that your network infrastructure can handle high volumes of traffic without bottlenecks. Consider implementing bandwidth management techniques, such as traffic shaping and QoS, to prioritize critical traffic and prevent congestion.

Redundancy and Failover

Redundancy is essential for maintaining the availability of your lab's network infrastructure. Implement redundant network paths, power supplies, and cooling systems to ensure that your lab remains operational even in the event of hardware failures. Additionally, consider using failover mechanisms to automatically switch to backup systems if the primary systems fail.

Virtualization Strategies for Scalability

Virtualization is a key enabler of scalability in offensive security labs. It allows you to run multiple VMs on a single physical server, making it easier to simulate complex environments and scale your lab as needed. Here are some virtualization strategies to consider:

Clustered Virtualization

Clustered virtualization involves grouping multiple physical servers into a single virtual cluster. This allows you to distribute VMs across multiple servers, balancing the load and providing redundancy. If one server in the cluster fails, the VMs can be automatically migrated to another server without downtime. Clustered virtualization is particularly useful for large-scale labs that require high availability and fault tolerance.

Dynamic Resource Allocation

Dynamic resource allocation allows virtualization platforms to automatically adjust the allocation of CPU, memory, and storage resources based on the needs of each VM. This ensures that resources are used efficiently and that VMs receive the resources they need to operate effectively. Dynamic resource allocation is essential for maintaining performance as the number of VMs in your lab increases.

Snapshot and Cloning

Snapshot and cloning features are useful for creating backups of VMs and quickly deploying new instances. Snapshots capture the state of a VM at a specific point in time, allowing you to revert to that state if needed. Cloning allows you to create exact copies of VMs, which can be useful for testing different configurations or running multiple instances of the same environment.

Containerization

Containerization is an alternative to traditional virtualization that allows you to run applications in isolated containers on a shared operating system. Containers are lightweight and can be deployed quickly, making them ideal for testing individual applications or services. Containerization platforms, such as Docker, provide a scalable way to deploy and manage applications within your lab environment.

Scaling Your Lab Over Time

As your organization's needs evolve, so too will the demands on your offensive security lab. To ensure that your lab remains scalable and effective, consider the following strategies for scaling over time:

Regular Capacity Planning

Conduct regular capacity planning exercises to assess your lab's current resources and anticipate future needs. This involves monitoring the utilization of CPU, memory, storage, and network bandwidth, and identifying potential bottlenecks. Based on the results, you can plan for hardware upgrades or adjustments to your lab's configuration.

Incremental Upgrades

Rather than making large, disruptive changes to your lab's infrastructure, consider implementing incremental upgrades. For example, you might add additional servers or storage devices as needed, rather than overhauling the entire infrastructure at once. Incremental upgrades allow you to scale your lab gradually, minimizing downtime and ensuring that your lab remains operational.

Automation and Orchestration

As your lab grows, automation becomes increasingly important for managing resources and workflows. Consider implementing automation and orchestration tools, such as Ansible, Puppet, or Kubernetes, to automate the deployment, configuration, and management of VMs and containers. Automation reduces the manual effort required to scale your lab and ensures consistency across environments.

Collaboration with Other Teams

Finally, consider collaborating with other teams within your organization, such as IT, DevOps, and security operations, to leverage their expertise and resources. Collaboration can help you identify new opportunities for scaling your lab and ensure that it aligns with the broader goals of the organization.

Conclusion

Designing a scalable lab infrastructure is essential for ensuring that your offensive security lab can grow and adapt to meet the evolving needs of your organization. By carefully selecting hardware, designing a flexible network infrastructure, and implementing effective virtualization strategies, you can create a lab environment that is both powerful and scalable. As your lab grows, regular capacity planning, incremental upgrades, and automation will help you maintain its effectiveness and ensure that it remains a valuable resource for your security team.

In the next chapter, we will explore the process of setting up a virtualized environment within your lab, including the configuration of VMs, networks, and storage to support a wide range of offensive security activities.

Chapter 6: Setting Up a Virtualized Environment

In the previous chapters, we discussed the importance of scalability and the selection of appropriate tools and technologies for your offensive security lab. Now, we turn our attention to the practical aspects of setting up a virtualized environment within your lab. A virtualized environment allows you to simulate complex network scenarios, create isolated test environments, and efficiently manage resources. In this chapter, we will cover the steps involved in setting up a virtualized environment, including the configuration of virtual machines (VMs), virtual networks, and storage.

Understanding Virtualization

Virtualization is the process of creating a virtual version of something, such as a server, a storage device, or a network resource. In the context of an offensive security lab, virtualization allows you to run multiple VMs on a single physical server, enabling you to simulate various operating systems, network topologies, and attack scenarios without the need for extensive physical hardware. Virtualization also offers flexibility, as VMs can be easily created, modified, and deleted, making it possible to test different configurations and scenarios with minimal effort.

There are several types of virtualization technologies available, including full virtualization, paravirtualization, and containerization. Each has its own strengths and use cases:

Full Virtualization: This approach uses a hypervisor to create and manage VMs, each of which runs its own complete operating system. Examples of hypervisors include VMware ESXi, Microsoft Hyper-V, and open-source solutions like KVM (Kernel-based Virtual Machine).

Paravirtualization: In this model, the guest operating systems are aware of the hypervisor and communicate directly with it for better performance. This method requires modified guest OS kernels, making it less common in general-purpose labs but useful in certain high-performance scenarios.

Containerization: Unlike traditional virtualization, containerization virtualizes the operating system rather than the hardware. Containers share the host OS kernel but run isolated processes, making them more lightweight and faster to deploy than traditional VMs. Docker is the most widely used containerization platform.

Setting Up Virtual Machines (VMs)

Virtual machines are the building blocks of a virtualized environment. Each VM runs its own operating system and applications, making it possible to simulate different endpoints, servers, and attack surfaces. Here's how to set up and configure VMs in your offensive security lab:

Choosing the Operating Systems

The first step is to choose the operating systems that will be installed on your VMs. Your selection should reflect the environments you intend to test. Common choices include:

Windows Servers and Workstations: For simulating enterprise environments.

Linux Distributions (e.g., Ubuntu, CentOS, Kali Linux): For servers, network appliances, or penetration testing tools.

MacOS: For testing against Apple environments, though this requires specific configurations due to Apple's hardware restrictions.

Installing the Hypervisor

The hypervisor is the software layer that allows you to create and manage VMs on a physical server. Install your chosen hypervisor on your lab's physical servers. Popular choices include:

VMware ESXi: A robust, enterprise-grade hypervisor that supports a wide range of features and integrations.

Microsoft Hyper-V: Integrated with Windows Server, Hyper-V is a good choice for organizations already using Microsoft technologies.

KVM: An open-source hypervisor that is highly customizable and integrates well with Linux environments.

Creating Virtual Machines

Once the hypervisor is installed, you can start creating VMs. Allocate resources (CPU, memory, storage) based on the needs of each VM. For instance, a VM simulating a web server might require more memory and CPU resources than a simple workstation. Most hypervisors offer templates or cloning features to quickly create multiple VMs with similar configurations.

Configuring VM Snapshots

Snapshots are a valuable feature of virtualization, allowing you to capture the state of a VM at a specific point in time. This is particularly useful in an offensive security lab, where you may want to revert to a previous state after testing an exploit or making significant changes to a VM's configuration. Configure regular snapshots of your VMs, especially before running potentially destructive tests.

Setting Up Guest Tools

Many hypervisors offer guest tools or additions that improve the performance and usability of VMs. These tools provide better integration between the VM and the host, including enhanced graphics, improved mouse integration, and optimized network performance. Install these tools on each VM to ensure smooth operation and better performance.

Configuring Virtual Networks

Virtual networks are essential for simulating real-world network scenarios within your lab. They allow you to create isolated networks, segmented environments, and complex topologies without the need for physical networking equipment. Here's how to configure virtual networks in your lab:

Designing the Network Topology

Start by designing the network topology that best suits your testing needs. Common topologies include:

Flat Network: All VMs are connected to a single virtual network, simulating a simple, unsegmented environment.

Segmented Network: VMs are connected to different segments, such as internal, DMZ, and external networks, allowing for more complex testing scenarios.

Isolated Network: VMs are placed in isolated networks with no external connectivity, useful for testing malware or other destructive activities.

Creating Virtual Switches

Virtual switches are used to connect VMs to each other and to the physical network. Most hypervisors allow you to create multiple virtual switches, each with its own configuration. Create virtual switches that correspond to your network topology, assigning VMs to the appropriate switches based on their role in the lab.

Configuring VLANs

Virtual LANs (VLANs) can be used to segment network traffic within a single virtual switch. This is useful for creating isolated environments or separating different types of traffic (e.g., management, production, testing). Configure VLANs on your virtual switches and assign VMs to the appropriate VLANs to control traffic flow within your lab.

Implementing Network Security Controls

Even in a lab environment, it's important to implement network security controls to prevent unintended consequences. Use virtual firewalls, intrusion detection/prevention systems (IDS/IPS), and other security devices to monitor and control traffic between VMs. This setup not only improves security but also allows you to test the effectiveness of these devices in various scenarios.

Setting Up VPNs and Tunnels

For scenarios that require remote access or testing across multiple locations, consider setting up VPNs or encrypted tunnels within your virtual network. This allows you to simulate attacks from external networks or to securely connect different segments of your lab.

Configuring Storage for Virtual Environments

Storage is a critical component of a virtualized environment, as it houses the VMs, snapshots, and associated data. Here are the key considerations for configuring storage in your lab:

Selecting Storage Types

Depending on your needs, you might use a combination of storage types:

Direct-Attached Storage (DAS): Storage devices directly connected to your physical servers. It's simple and cost-effective but offers limited scalability.

Network-Attached Storage (NAS): A dedicated storage device connected to your network, providing centralized storage for all VMs. NAS devices are easy to manage and offer better scalability.

Storage Area Network (SAN): A high-performance, dedicated network for storage devices, offering the best performance and scalability for large labs.

Configuring Storage Pools

Most hypervisors allow you to create storage pools—aggregations of storage resources that can be allocated to different VMs. Create storage pools based on the performance and capacity needs of your VMs. For instance, high-performance applications might require storage pools with SSDs, while less demanding applications can use HDD-based pools.

Managing Disk Images and Snapshots

Disk images are the virtual hard drives used by your VMs. Manage these images carefully to optimize performance and storage usage. Regularly clean up old snapshots and unused disk images to free up storage space. Consider implementing thin provisioning, which allows disk images to use only the storage they need, rather than reserving the entire allocated space upfront.

Backup and Disaster Recovery

Even in a lab environment, it's important to have a backup and disaster recovery plan. Regularly back up your VMs, snapshots, and critical configurations to ensure that you can recover quickly from hardware failures, data corruption, or accidental deletions. Store backups in a separate location or on a different storage device to protect against data loss.

Testing and Validation

Once your virtualized environment is set up, it's crucial to test and validate the configuration to ensure that everything is working as expected. Conduct a series of tests to verify that:

VMs are Functioning Properly: Ensure that each VM boots correctly, has the necessary resources, and can communicate with other VMs and the physical network.

Network Traffic is Flowing as Intended: Test your virtual networks to ensure that traffic is flowing according to your design. This includes verifying VLAN configurations, firewall rules, and any network segmentation.

Storage is Performing Optimally: Check that your storage devices are providing the expected performance and that your VMs have access to the necessary storage resources.

Security Controls are Effective: Verify that your virtual firewalls, IDS/IPS, and other security controls are detecting and blocking unauthorized traffic or attacks within the lab environment.

Conclusion

Setting up a virtualized environment is a fundamental step in building a flexible and scalable offensive security lab. By carefully configuring virtual machines, networks, and storage, you can create a powerful testing environment that simulates real-world scenarios while maintaining control and security. This virtualized environment will serve as the backbone of your lab, enabling you to test, refine, and develop advanced security strategies.

In the next chapter, we will explore the process of deploying network architectures within your lab, including the configuration of complex topologies, routing, and network services to support a wide range of offensive security activities.

Chapter 7: Deploying Network Architectures

With the virtualized environment in place, the next step in building your offensive security lab is to deploy network architectures that support various testing scenarios. Network architecture is the blueprint of how network devices, systems, and services are interconnected. A well-designed network architecture allows you to simulate different types of networks, from simple home setups to complex enterprise environments, providing a realistic context for your security assessments. In this chapter, we will cover the principles of network architecture, the configuration of routing and switching, and the deployment of network services in your lab.

Understanding Network Architecture Design

Network architecture refers to the structural design of a network, including the arrangement of its components (routers, switches, firewalls, etc.) and the protocols that govern data flow. When designing network architecture for an offensive security lab, consider the following principles:

Modularity: Design your network in modules that can be independently managed and scaled. Common modules include internal networks, external networks, DMZs, and management networks. Modularity simplifies troubleshooting and allows for targeted testing of specific network segments.

Scalability: Ensure that the network architecture can scale as the number of devices and complexity of testing scenarios increase. This includes planning for additional routers, switches, and links as needed.

Redundancy: Incorporate redundancy to improve network availability and resilience. This includes redundant paths, devices, and power supplies to ensure that your network remains operational even in the event of failures.

Security: Design your network with security in mind. This includes segmenting networks based on security requirements, implementing firewalls and access controls, and using encryption for sensitive traffic.

Flexibility: Your network architecture should be flexible enough to support a wide range of testing scenarios, from simple vulnerability scans to advanced persistent threat simulations. This flexibility can be achieved through the use of VLANs, VPNs, and software-defined networking (SDN) technologies.

Configuring Routing and Switching

Routing and switching are the core functions of any network, determining how data is forwarded from one device to another. In an offensive security lab, proper configuration of routing and switching is essential for creating realistic and functional network topologies.

Switch Configuration

Switches are used to connect devices within the same network segment. In your lab, switches can be either physical or virtual, depending on your setup. Here's how to configure your switches:

VLANs: Use VLANs to segment your network into different logical groups. For example, you might create separate VLANs for management, production, and testing traffic. Configure the switch ports to tag traffic with the appropriate VLAN IDs.

Port Security: Implement port security features to control which devices can connect to the switch. This can include MAC address filtering or limiting the number of devices on a single port.

Trunking: Configure trunk ports to allow VLAN traffic to pass between switches. Trunking is essential for connecting different segments of your lab's network.

Router Configuration

Routers are responsible for forwarding packets between different networks. In your lab, routers can be used to connect VLANs, create DMZs, and simulate external networks. Here's how to configure your routers:

Static Routing: For simple networks, static routes can be used to manually define the path that traffic takes between networks. This is easy to configure but lacks flexibility for larger networks.

Dynamic Routing: For more complex networks, consider using dynamic routing protocols like OSPF (Open Shortest Path First) or BGP (Border Gateway Protocol). These protocols automatically adjust routing paths based on network changes, providing greater flexibility.

Access Control Lists (ACLs): Use ACLs to control traffic flow between networks. ACLs can be used to permit or deny specific types of traffic, providing an additional layer of security.

Firewall Configuration

Firewalls are critical for protecting your network and controlling traffic flow. In your lab, firewalls can be used to create isolated environments, simulate DMZs, and enforce security policies. Here's how to configure your firewalls:

Firewall Rules: Define rules that control which traffic is allowed or denied between network segments. For example, you might allow HTTP and HTTPS traffic to pass from the DMZ to the internal network but block all other traffic.

NAT (Network Address Translation): Use NAT to translate private IP addresses to public IP addresses. This is useful for simulating scenarios where internal resources need to communicate with external networks.

VPNs and Tunnels: Configure VPNs or encrypted tunnels on your firewall to simulate remote access scenarios or connect different segments of your lab securely.

Deploying Network Services

Network services provide the necessary infrastructure for communication, security, and management within your lab. These services can include DNS, DHCP, VPNs, and more. Here's how to deploy and configure essential network services in your lab:

DNS (Domain Name System)

DNS is responsible for translating domain names into IP addresses. In your lab, you can set up a DNS server to simulate internal and external DNS resolution. This is particularly useful for testing phishing attacks, domain hijacking, or other DNS-based threats.

Primary and Secondary DNS Servers: Set up both primary and secondary DNS servers for redundancy. Ensure that your DNS configuration includes forward and reverse lookup zones.

DNSSEC (DNS Security Extensions): Consider implementing DNSSEC to test scenarios involving DNS security. DNSSEC adds an additional layer of security by enabling DNS responses to be authenticated.

DHCP (Dynamic Host Configuration Protocol)

DHCP is used to automatically assign IP addresses and other network configuration details to devices. Setting up a DHCP server in your lab simplifies the management of IP addresses and ensures that devices can connect to the network seamlessly.

Scope Configuration: Define IP address scopes for each network segment. Ensure that scopes do not overlap and that the range of IP addresses is sufficient for the number of devices in each segment.

Reservations and Options: Use DHCP reservations to assign specific IP addresses to critical devices. Configure DHCP options to automatically provide clients with DNS server addresses, default gateways, and other settings.

VPN (Virtual Private Network)

VPNs are used to create secure connections between different parts of your lab or to simulate remote access scenarios. Deploying a VPN server in your lab allows you to test the security and performance of VPN connections.

Site-to-Site VPN: Use site-to-site VPNs to connect different network segments securely. This is useful for simulating scenarios where different parts of an organization's network are connected over a public network.

Client-to-Site VPN: Set up client-to-site VPNs to simulate remote access by individual users. Test the security of VPN connections, including encryption strength and vulnerability to attacks.

Proxy Servers

Proxy servers are used to control and monitor traffic between clients and external networks. In your lab, proxy servers can be used to test content filtering, anonymization, and other security measures.

Web Proxy: Set up a web proxy to filter and cache web traffic. Test scenarios involving content filtering, malware detection, and anonymous browsing.

Reverse Proxy: Use a reverse proxy to handle requests from external clients to internal servers. This is useful for load balancing, SSL termination, and hiding internal server details from attackers.

Testing and Validation

Once your network architecture is deployed, it's essential to test and validate the configuration to ensure that everything is functioning as expected. Conduct a series of tests to verify:

Connectivity: Ensure that all devices can communicate as intended, both within the same network segment and across different segments. Use tools like ping, traceroute, and telnet to test connectivity.

Security: Test your firewall rules, ACLs, and other security controls to ensure they are correctly configured. Attempt to bypass these controls to identify any weaknesses.

Performance: Measure the performance of your network to ensure that it can handle the expected load. Use tools like iPerf to test bandwidth and latency, and consider simulating high-traffic scenarios to test the network's resilience.

Service Availability: Verify that all network services (DNS, DHCP, VPNs, etc.) are functioning correctly and that they can handle the expected number of clients. Test failover scenarios to ensure that redundancy mechanisms are working as intended.

Conclusion

Deploying network architectures in your offensive security lab is a critical step in creating a realistic and functional testing environment. By carefully designing your network topology, configuring routing and switching, and deploying essential network services, you can create a lab environment that supports a wide range of testing scenarios. This will enable your team to simulate real-world attacks, test defense mechanisms, and develop effective security strategies.

In the next chapter, we will explore how to integrate threat intelligence platforms into your lab environment, allowing you to simulate the latest threats and enhance the realism of your testing scenarios.

Chapter 8: Integrating Threat Intelligence Platforms

Integrating threat intelligence platforms into your offensive security lab is a crucial step in enhancing the realism and effectiveness of your testing scenarios. Threat intelligence provides valuable insights into the tactics, techniques, and procedures (TTPs) used by real-world attackers, enabling your team to simulate current and emerging threats accurately. In this chapter, we will explore the importance of threat intelligence, how to select and integrate a threat intelligence platform (TIP) into your lab, and ways to use this intelligence to inform your security assessments and training.

Understanding Threat Intelligence

Threat intelligence is the process of gathering, analyzing, and applying information about current and potential threats to an organization. This intelligence can come from a variety of sources, including open-source data, commercial feeds, and information sharing between organizations. Threat intelligence helps security teams understand the motivations and methods of attackers, identify potential vulnerabilities, and develop strategies to defend against specific threats.

There are three main types of threat intelligence:

Strategic Intelligence: High-level information about overall trends and threat landscapes, often used by executives and decision-makers to guide security policies and investments.

Operational Intelligence: Information about specific campaigns, attack methods, and threat actors. This type of intelligence is used to identify and respond to threats that are actively targeting an organization.

Tactical Intelligence: Detailed technical information, such as indicators of compromise (IOCs), attack signatures, and exploit details. Tactical intelligence is used by security teams to detect and mitigate specific threats in real-time.

By integrating threat intelligence into your offensive security lab, you can create more realistic and relevant testing scenarios, ensuring that your security assessments are aligned with the current threat landscape.

Selecting a Threat Intelligence Platform (TIP)

A threat intelligence platform (TIP) is a tool that aggregates, analyzes, and disseminates threat intelligence from various sources. A good TIP allows you to centralize your threat data, correlate it with your environment, and automate the application of intelligence to your security operations. Here are some key considerations for selecting a TIP:

Data Sources: The TIP should support integration with multiple data sources, including open-source intelligence (OSINT), commercial threat feeds, internal logs, and information-sharing communities like ISACs (Information Sharing and Analysis Centers). The more diverse the data sources, the more comprehensive your threat intelligence will be.

Analysis Capabilities: Look for a TIP that offers advanced analysis features, such as machine learning, behavioral analysis, and correlation engines. These features help identify patterns, link related threats, and prioritize intelligence based on the potential impact.

Integration with Security Tools: The TIP should integrate seamlessly with your existing security tools, such as SIEM (Security Information and Event Management) systems, intrusion detection/prevention systems (IDS/IPS), and firewalls. This integration allows you to automate the application of threat intelligence and respond to threats more effectively.

Customization and Flexibility: Choose a TIP that allows you to customize its features and workflows to meet your specific needs. This includes the ability to create custom dashboards, set up alerts, and define how intelligence is used in your lab environment.

User Interface and Usability: The TIP should have a user-friendly interface that makes it easy to navigate, analyze data, and generate reports. A steep learning curve can hinder your team's ability to quickly leverage the platform's capabilities.

Support and Community: Consider the level of support and the size of the user community when selecting a TIP. A strong community can provide valuable insights, shared experiences, and best practices, while good vendor support ensures you can resolve any issues quickly.

Integrating the TIP into Your Lab Environment

Once you have selected a TIP, the next step is to integrate it into your offensive security lab. This involves configuring the platform, connecting it to your data sources, and setting up workflows that allow you to use the intelligence in your security assessments. Here's how to do it:

Configuring the Platform

Begin by installing the TIP on a dedicated server or VM within your lab environment. Ensure that the server has sufficient resources (CPU, memory, storage) to handle the volume of data that the TIP will process. During installation, configure the TIP to align with your lab's network architecture, ensuring it has access to the necessary data sources and can communicate with other tools in your lab.

Connecting Data Sources

The effectiveness of a TIP depends on the quality and diversity of the data it ingests. Connect the TIP to various data sources, including:

Open-Source Intelligence (OSINT): Integrate feeds from publicly available sources like threat research blogs, security advisories, and repositories like VirusTotal and Shodan.

Commercial Threat Feeds: If you subscribe to commercial threat intelligence services, configure the TIP to ingest data from these feeds. Commercial feeds often provide high-fidelity intelligence, including zero-day vulnerabilities and nation-state actor activity.

Internal Logs and Telemetry: Connect the TIP to your internal log sources, such as SIEM systems, IDS/IPS logs, and firewall logs. This allows you to correlate external threat intelligence with events occurring in your environment.

Information Sharing Communities: Join relevant ISACs or industry-specific information-sharing groups and integrate their intelligence feeds into your TIP.

Setting Up Intelligence Workflows

Once the TIP is configured and connected to data sources, set up workflows that automate the application of threat intelligence within your lab. These workflows might include:

Automated Enrichment: Automatically enrich security alerts and events with relevant threat intelligence, providing additional context for your team to make informed decisions.

Threat Hunting: Use the TIP to identify patterns and indicators of compromise (IOCs) that match known threats. This can involve searching through logs, network traffic, and endpoint data for signs of malicious activity.

Incident Response: Integrate the TIP with your incident response processes, allowing your team to quickly access relevant intelligence during an investigation. This can help prioritize response actions and identify the root cause of an incident.

Reporting and Alerting: Set up automated reports and alerts that notify your team of new or high-priority threats. This ensures that your team stays informed of emerging threats and can take proactive measures to defend against them.

Testing and Validation

After setting up the TIP and its workflows, it's essential to test and validate the integration to ensure that it is functioning correctly. Conduct tests to verify:

Data Ingestion: Confirm that the TIP is successfully ingesting data from all configured sources and that the data is being processed and correlated correctly.

Automation: Test the automation workflows to ensure that they are triggering as expected and providing actionable intelligence to your team.

Integration with Security Tools: Verify that the TIP is properly integrated with your other security tools and that intelligence is being applied effectively across your lab environment.

Using Threat Intelligence in Security Assessments

With the TIP fully integrated into your lab, you can begin using threat intelligence to inform your security assessments. Here are some ways to leverage this intelligence in your testing and training activities:

Simulating Real-World Attacks

Use the intelligence gathered by your TIP to simulate real-world attacks within your lab environment. This can involve replicating the tactics, techniques, and procedures (TTPs) used by specific threat actors, as well as testing your defenses against these scenarios. By simulating the latest threats, you can ensure that your security measures are effective and up to date.

Identifying Vulnerabilities

Use threat intelligence to identify vulnerabilities in your environment that are being actively exploited by attackers. This can involve correlating intelligence on known vulnerabilities with your own asset inventory and prioritizing remediation efforts based on the risk level.

Training and Skill Development

Incorporate threat intelligence into your training programs to help your security team stay current on emerging threats and attack methods. This can involve creating realistic training scenarios based on recent attacks, as well as conducting red team exercises that challenge your team to defend against simulated threats.

Threat Hunting

Conduct proactive threat hunting exercises using the intelligence provided by your TIP. This involves searching for signs of compromise within your lab environment that may have gone undetected by traditional security measures. Threat hunting allows you to identify and mitigate potential threats before they can cause significant damage.

Enhancing Incident Response

During incident response exercises, use the intelligence from your TIP to guide your investigation and response efforts. This can help you quickly identify the source of an attack, understand the tactics used by the attacker, and determine the best course of action to contain and remediate the threat.

Conclusion

Integrating a threat intelligence platform into your offensive security lab is a powerful way to enhance the realism and effectiveness of your security assessments. By centralizing, analyzing, and applying intelligence from multiple sources, you can simulate real-world threats, identify vulnerabilities, and develop more effective defense strategies. With the TIP fully integrated into your lab, you can stay ahead of emerging threats and ensure that your security team is prepared to defend against the latest attacks.

In the next chapter, we will explore how to simulate advanced persistent threats (APTs) within your lab environment, using the intelligence gathered to test your organization's defenses against sophisticated and persistent attackers.

Chapter 9: Simulating Advanced Persistent Threats (APTs)

Advanced Persistent Threats (APTs) represent some of the most dangerous and sophisticated cyber threats facing organizations today. Unlike typical cyber attacks that are often quick and opportunistic, APTs involve prolonged and targeted efforts to infiltrate a network, often with the goal of stealing sensitive information or disrupting critical operations. Simulating APTs in your offensive security lab is essential for understanding how these threats operate and for developing strategies to defend against them. In this chapter, we will explore the characteristics of APTs, how to design and simulate APT scenarios in your lab, and how to assess and improve your defenses against such threats.

Understanding Advanced Persistent Threats (APTs)

APTs are characterized by their complexity, persistence, and stealth. These attacks are usually carried out by well-funded and highly skilled adversaries, such as nation-state actors, organized crime groups, or corporate espionage agents. The objectives of APTs vary but often include the theft of intellectual property, espionage, or the disruption of critical infrastructure.

Key characteristics of APTs include:

Targeted Attacks: APTs are typically aimed at specific organizations or industries, often with a strategic objective in mind. The attackers invest significant time and resources to understand the target's environment and to develop customized attack vectors.

Stealth and Evasion: APTs are designed to remain undetected for extended periods. Attackers use sophisticated techniques to evade detection, such as encryption, polymorphic malware, and lateral movement within the network.

Persistence: Once inside a network, APT actors maintain their presence over the long term. They often establish multiple footholds and use various methods to regain access if one entry point is discovered and closed.

Multi-Stage Attacks: APTs often involve multiple stages, including initial compromise, escalation of privileges, lateral movement, and exfiltration of data. Each stage is carefully planned and executed to achieve the attackers' objectives.

Advanced Tactics and Techniques: APT actors use a wide range of advanced tactics, techniques, and procedures (TTPs), often blending custom-built tools with legitimate software to avoid detection. These may include zero-day exploits, social engineering, spear-phishing, and sophisticated malware.

Given these characteristics, defending against APTs requires a deep understanding of the attackers' methods and a proactive approach to security. Simulating APTs in your lab allows you to test your defenses, identify weaknesses, and develop strategies to protect against these advanced threats.

Designing an APT Simulation

Simulating an APT in your lab involves creating a realistic scenario that mimics the methods and objectives of a real-world APT. The goal is to test your organization's ability to detect, respond to, and mitigate an advanced and persistent attack. Here's how to design an effective APT simulation:

Define the Attack Scenario

Start by defining the scope and objectives of the APT simulation. Consider the following elements:

Target Selection: Identify the systems, applications, or data that will be the focus of the APT simulation. This could include critical infrastructure, intellectual property, or sensitive customer data.

Attack Objectives: Define the objectives of the simulated APT. This could involve data exfiltration, disruption of services, or gaining long-term control over the target environment.

Adversary Emulation: Choose an adversary profile to emulate during the simulation. This could be based on a known APT group, such as APT28 or APT29, with specific TTPs that align with the group's historical behavior.

Develop the Attack Chain

APTs typically involve a multi-stage attack chain, also known as the kill chain. Design the attack chain for your simulation, including each stage that the attackers will go through to achieve their objectives. Common stages include:

Reconnaissance: Gathering information about the target environment, such as network architecture, employee roles, and software versions.

Initial Compromise: Gaining access to the target network through methods like spear-phishing, watering hole attacks, or exploiting vulnerabilities.

Establishing Persistence: Installing backdoors or malware that allow the attackers to maintain access to the network.

Privilege Escalation: Gaining higher levels of access within the network, such as administrative privileges, to move freely across systems.

Lateral Movement: Moving laterally within the network to identify and access high-value targets, such as file servers, databases, or email accounts.

Data Exfiltration: Extracting sensitive data from the network, often using encrypted channels or covert methods to avoid detection.

Cleanup: Covering tracks by deleting logs, removing malware, and disabling forensic tools to make detection and investigation more difficult.

Select Tools and Techniques

Based on the attack chain, select the tools and techniques that will be used in the simulation. These should be aligned with the TTPs of the adversary you are emulating. Common tools and techniques include:

Malware Development: Custom-built or modified malware that is designed to bypass your organization's defenses.

Exploit Kits: Exploit kits that target known vulnerabilities in software or hardware used by the target environment.

Command and Control (C2): Setting up C2 infrastructure to control compromised systems remotely and exfiltrate data.

Social Engineering: Phishing campaigns, pretexting, or other social engineering tactics to trick employees into providing access or information.

Establish Metrics for Success

To evaluate the effectiveness of your simulation, establish metrics for success. These metrics should include both detection and response times, as well as the impact of the simulated attack. Common metrics include:

Time to Detection: How long it takes for your security team to detect the initial compromise or any subsequent stages of the attack.

Time to Containment: How quickly your team can contain the attack once it is detected, including isolating compromised systems and blocking further access.

Impact on Operations: The extent to which the simulated APT affects your organization's operations, such as downtime, data loss, or disruption of services.

Executing the APT Simulation

Once the APT simulation is designed, the next step is to execute it within your lab environment. This involves launching the attack, monitoring the response, and gathering data for analysis. Here's how to carry out the simulation:

Launch the Attack

Begin the simulation by launching the initial stages of the attack. This could involve sending spear-phishing emails, exploiting vulnerabilities, or deploying malware on targeted systems. Ensure that the attack progresses through each stage of the kill chain, with the attackers adapting to any defenses encountered.

Monitor the Response

As the attack unfolds, monitor your organization's response. This includes tracking how quickly the security team detects the attack, what actions they take to contain it, and how effectively they mitigate its impact. Use your lab's monitoring and logging tools to capture detailed data on the attack's progression and the response efforts.

Record Observations and Gather Data

Throughout the simulation, record your observations and gather data on key metrics, such as detection times, response times, and the success of different defense mechanisms. Pay attention to any gaps or weaknesses in your defenses that the attackers are able to exploit.

Simulate Adversary Adaptation

One of the hallmarks of APTs is the ability of attackers to adapt to changing circumstances. During the simulation, introduce challenges that force the attackers to adapt, such as activating additional security controls or changing network configurations. Observe how the attackers respond and whether they can maintain their presence in the network.

End the Simulation

Once the attack objectives are achieved or the security team successfully contains the threat, end the simulation. Ensure that all systems and data are restored to their pre-simulation state and that any changes made during the attack are documented for analysis.

Analyzing the Results

After the simulation is complete, the next step is to analyze the results and identify areas for improvement. This involves reviewing the data collected during the simulation, assessing the effectiveness of your defenses, and developing recommendations for enhancing your security posture. Here's how to analyze the results:

Review Key Metrics

Start by reviewing the key metrics you established before the simulation, such as detection times, response times, and operational impact. Identify any areas where the security team performed well and any areas where improvements are needed.

Identify Gaps and Weaknesses

Analyze the attack chain to identify any gaps or weaknesses in your defenses that the attackers were able to exploit. This could include vulnerabilities that were not patched, insufficient monitoring, or delays in the response process.

Assess the Effectiveness of Security Controls

Evaluate the effectiveness of the security controls that were in place during the simulation. This includes firewalls, intrusion detection/prevention systems (IDS/IPS), endpoint protection, and any other defenses used to detect and mitigate the attack. Identify any controls that failed to perform as expected and determine why.

Develop Recommendations

Based on the analysis, develop recommendations for improving your organization's defenses against APTs. This could include implementing additional security controls, improving monitoring and detection capabilities, or enhancing incident response procedures. Consider both short-term actions that can be implemented quickly and long-term strategies for strengthening your overall security posture.

Conduct a Debriefing

Hold a debriefing session with the security team to discuss the results of the simulation. Review what went well and what could be improved, and encourage team members to share their observations and insights. Use this feedback to refine your security strategy and to plan future simulations.

Continuous Improvement

Simulating APTs is not a one-time exercise; it should be part of a continuous process of improvement. As new threats emerge and your organization's environment evolves, regularly update your APT simulations to reflect current risks. Use the insights gained from each simulation to make incremental improvements to your defenses and to ensure that your security team is always prepared to respond to the latest threats.

Conclusion

Simulating Advanced Persistent Threats in your offensive security lab is a critical step in understanding and defending against these sophisticated and dangerous attacks. By designing realistic APT scenarios, executing detailed simulations, and analyzing the results, you can identify weaknesses in your defenses, improve your security posture, and ensure that your organization is prepared to face the most advanced threats. As the threat landscape continues to evolve, maintaining a proactive approach to security through continuous simulation and improvement will be essential to staying ahead of potential adversaries.

In the next chapter, we will explore the development of custom exploits and payloads, a key aspect of offensive security that allows you to test your defenses against unique and emerging threats.

Chapter 10: Developing Custom Exploits and Payloads

The ability to develop custom exploits and payloads is a critical skill in offensive security. While many tools and exploits are available off the shelf, advanced adversaries often create their own custom exploits to bypass defenses and achieve their objectives. By developing your own custom exploits and payloads in a controlled lab environment, you can better understand how these attacks work, test your defenses against novel threats, and prepare your security team for the kinds of challenges they may face in the real world. In this chapter, we will explore the fundamentals of exploit development, the process of creating custom payloads, and how to safely test these creations within your offensive security lab.

Understanding Exploit Development

An exploit is a piece of code or a sequence of commands that takes advantage of a vulnerability in software, hardware, or a network protocol to achieve unauthorized actions on a target system. Exploit development involves identifying a vulnerability, understanding its mechanics, and crafting code that can reliably trigger the vulnerability to achieve the desired effect, such as gaining remote access, escalating privileges, or executing arbitrary code.

There are several stages in the exploit development process:

Vulnerability Identification: The first step in exploit development is identifying a vulnerability in a target system. Vulnerabilities can be found in various ways, including through manual code review, fuzzing (automated testing for unexpected inputs), or analyzing patch updates for known software.

Exploit Research: Once a vulnerability is identified, the next step is to understand how it can be exploited. This involves analyzing the vulnerability to determine how it affects the system, what conditions are necessary to trigger it, and what the potential impacts are.

Exploit Coding: After the research phase, the actual development of the exploit begins. This involves writing code that triggers the vulnerability in a controlled manner. The code must be carefully crafted to avoid crashing the system or causing unintended side effects.

Testing and Refinement: The exploit must be tested extensively to ensure that it works reliably across different environments and configurations. This phase often involves refining the code to handle edge cases and improve its effectiveness.

Payload Integration: Once the exploit is working, a payload is integrated into it. The payload is the part of the exploit that executes the desired action on the target system, such as opening a backdoor, exfiltrating data, or disabling security measures.

Obfuscation and Evasion: To avoid detection by security tools, many exploits undergo obfuscation—techniques used to make the exploit code harder to analyze or detect. This might involve encoding the payload, using polymorphic techniques to change the exploit's appearance, or employing encryption to hide the exploit's functionality.

Tools and Environments for Exploit Development

Exploit development requires specialized tools and a controlled environment to ensure safety and effectiveness. Here are some of the key tools and environments used in the process:

Debuggers: Debuggers are essential for analyzing how software behaves when an exploit is executed. Tools like GDB (GNU Debugger) for Linux and WinDbg for Windows allow you to step through code, inspect memory, and understand how a vulnerability is triggered.

Disassemblers and Decompilers: Tools like IDA Pro and Ghidra are used to disassemble or decompile binaries, providing a readable view of compiled code. This is crucial for reverse engineering and understanding the inner workings of a target application.

Fuzzers: Fuzzing tools like AFL (American Fuzzy Lop) and LibFuzzer are used to automatically test applications with random or malformed inputs to discover vulnerabilities. Fuzzers can be particularly effective at finding edge cases that lead to crashes or unexpected behavior.

Virtual Machines and Sandboxes: A safe environment is necessary to develop and test exploits. Virtual machines (VMs) provide isolated environments where you can execute exploits without risking damage to your production systems. Sandboxes like Cuckoo Sandbox allow you to observe the behavior of malware and exploits in a controlled setting.

Metasploit Framework: Metasploit is a widely-used penetration testing framework that includes tools for exploit development. It provides a platform to develop, test, and deploy exploits and payloads, making it easier to integrate custom code into a larger testing strategy.

Hex Editors: Tools like HxD allow you to view and edit binary files at the byte level, which can be useful for modifying payloads, patching binaries, or crafting shellcode.

Developing Custom Payloads

A payload is the component of an exploit that performs the desired action on the target system once the vulnerability is triggered. Custom payloads are often developed to achieve specific goals or to evade detection by security tools. Here's how to develop and integrate custom payloads:

Determine the Payload Objective

Before developing a payload, define its objective. Common payload objectives include:

Reverse Shell: Opens a command shell on the target system and connects back to the attacker's machine, allowing remote control.

Bind Shell: Opens a command shell on the target system and listens for incoming connections from the attacker.

File Download and Execute: Downloads and executes a file from a remote server, often used to deploy secondary malware or tools.

Privilege Escalation: Elevates the privileges of the current user, allowing the attacker to perform actions that require higher permissions.

Data Exfiltration: Extracts sensitive data from the target system and sends it to the attacker.

Choose the Appropriate Language

Payloads can be written in various programming languages, depending on the target environment and the nature of the payload. Common choices include:

C/C++: Often used for low-level payloads that require direct interaction with the operating system or hardware.

Python: Useful for developing cross-platform payloads and for rapid prototyping. Python can be used in conjunction with tools like PyInstaller to create standalone executables.

PowerShell: Commonly used for Windows payloads, especially for fileless attacks that execute entirely in memory.

Assembly: Used for writing shellcode, the smallest and most direct form of payload, often used in buffer overflow exploits.

Writing the Payload

Develop the payload based on the chosen objective and language. Ensure that the payload is lightweight and efficient, as it may need to execute quickly and without leaving a trace. If you're writing shellcode, it's essential to keep the code small and avoid null bytes, as these can terminate strings and cause the payload to fail.

Encoding and Obfuscation

To evade detection by security tools, consider encoding or obfuscating the payload. Common techniques include:

Base64 Encoding: A simple method of encoding binary data into ASCII characters, often used to bypass filters that block binary content.

XOR Encoding: A basic encryption technique that uses an XOR operation with a key to obscure the payload's contents.

Polymorphism: Alters the payload's appearance by changing its code structure without affecting its functionality. This can be done automatically using tools like msfvenom within Metasploit.

Testing the Payload

Once the payload is developed, it's crucial to test it in a controlled environment to ensure it works as intended. This involves:

Testing in Virtual Machines: Execute the payload in a virtual machine to observe its behavior and ensure it achieves its objective without crashing or being detected.

Behavioral Analysis: Use sandbox tools to analyze how the payload interacts with the target system, including any files it modifies, processes it spawns, or network connections it makes.

Evasion Testing: Test the payload against various security tools, such as antivirus software, endpoint detection and response (EDR) solutions, and intrusion detection/prevention systems (IDS/IPS), to evaluate its ability to evade detection.

Integrating with Exploits

After testing, the custom payload can be integrated with an exploit. This involves modifying the exploit code to include the payload, ensuring that the payload is delivered and executed correctly when the vulnerability is triggered.

Safely Testing Exploits and Payloads

Testing custom exploits and payloads in a lab environment requires strict safety measures to avoid unintended consequences, such as accidental network compromise or data loss. Here are some best practices for safe testing:

Isolated Environment

Always conduct testing in an isolated environment, such as a virtualized lab, to ensure that any harmful effects of the exploit or payload are contained. Use network segmentation to prevent the exploit from spreading beyond the test environment.

Backup and Restore

Before testing, create snapshots or backups of your virtual machines and network configurations. This allows you to quickly restore the environment to a known good state if something goes wrong during testing.

Logging and Monitoring

Enable detailed logging and monitoring within your lab environment to capture all activities related to the exploit and payload. This data is invaluable for analyzing the effectiveness of the exploit and identifying any unexpected behavior.

Ethical Considerations

Ensure that all exploit and payload development is conducted ethically and within the bounds of legal and organizational guidelines. Unauthorized use of exploits and payloads can lead to legal consequences and harm to individuals or organizations.

Conclusion

Developing custom exploits and payloads is a challenging but essential aspect of offensive security. By mastering these skills, you can better understand how advanced threats operate, test your defenses against novel attacks, and enhance your ability to respond to emerging threats. In your lab environment, you have the opportunity to experiment, refine your techniques, and build a deep knowledge of the inner workings of exploits and payloads. As you continue to develop and test your creations, always prioritize safety, ethical considerations, and continuous learning.

In the next chapter, we will delve into the strategies and tactics of red team operations, where custom exploits and payloads play a central role in simulating real-world attacks against an organization's defenses.

Chapter 11: Red Team Operations: Strategies and Tactics

Red team operations are a critical component of an organization's offensive security strategy. Unlike traditional penetration testing, which often has a narrow focus on identifying specific vulnerabilities, red team operations simulate full-scale attacks that mimic real-world adversaries. These operations are designed to test an organization's overall security posture, including its ability to detect, respond to, and recover from advanced threats. In this chapter, we will explore the strategies and tactics used in red team operations, the planning and execution of these operations, and how to assess and improve an organization's defenses based on the findings.

Understanding Red Team Operations

Red team operations are designed to challenge an organization's defenses by simulating an adversary's actions. The goal is not just to find vulnerabilities but to test the entire security ecosystem, including people, processes, and technology. Red teamers adopt the mindset of attackers, using the same tactics, techniques, and procedures (TTPs) that real-world adversaries would use to compromise an organization.

Key characteristics of red team operations include:

Adversary Emulation: Red teams aim to emulate the behavior of specific adversaries, such as nation-state actors, cybercriminals, or hacktivists. This involves researching the TTPs associated with these adversaries and incorporating them into the operation.

Goal-Oriented: Red team operations are typically goal-oriented, with specific objectives such as stealing sensitive data, compromising critical systems, or maintaining persistent access within the network. The success of the operation is measured by the team's ability to achieve these objectives without being detected or stopped.

Comprehensive Scope: Unlike traditional penetration tests, which may focus on specific systems or applications, red team operations often have a broader scope. They may include network infrastructure, web applications, physical security, social engineering, and more.

Stealth and Persistence: Red teams prioritize stealth, aiming to avoid detection by the organization's defenses. They may use techniques such as lateral movement, privilege escalation, and persistence mechanisms to maintain access over an extended period.

Collaboration with Blue Teams: While red teams focus on simulating attacks, their ultimate goal is to improve the organization's defenses. Red team operations often involve collaboration with blue teams (the defenders) to help them identify weaknesses, improve detection capabilities, and develop better response strategies.

Planning Red Team Operations

Successful red team operations require careful planning and coordination. The planning phase involves defining the objectives, selecting the appropriate strategies and tactics, and establishing the rules of engagement. Here's how to plan an effective red team operation:

Define Objectives and Scope

Start by defining the objectives of the red team operation. These objectives should align with the organization's security goals and may include:

Testing Detection and Response: Assessing the organization's ability to detect and respond to an advanced threat.

Evaluating Defense-in-Depth: Testing the effectiveness of layered security controls and identifying gaps.

Simulating a Specific Adversary: Emulating the TTPs of a known adversary group to see how well the organization can defend against their tactics.

Once the objectives are defined, determine the scope of the operation. This includes identifying the systems, networks, applications, and physical locations that will be in-scope for the operation. Consider any restrictions or limitations, such as areas that are off-limits due to operational sensitivity or regulatory concerns.

Develop a Threat Model

A threat model helps identify potential attack vectors and the methods an adversary might use to achieve their objectives. Develop a threat model based on the adversary you are emulating, considering factors such as:

Entry Points: How might the adversary gain initial access to the organization? This could include phishing, exploiting vulnerabilities, or leveraging insider threats.

Targets: What systems, data, or assets are of interest to the adversary? Consider both high-value targets (e.g., domain controllers) and less obvious targets (e.g., employee credentials).

Attack Paths: What paths might the adversary take to move laterally within the network? Identify potential pivot points, such as shared folders, databases, or compromised accounts.

Persistence Mechanisms: How might the adversary maintain access over time? Consider the use of backdoors, malware, or compromised credentials.

Select Tactics, Techniques, and Procedures (TTPs)

Based on the threat model, select the TTPs that will be used during the operation. This involves choosing specific attack techniques, such as:

Spear-Phishing: Crafting targeted phishing emails to gain initial access or harvest credentials.

Exploitation: Identifying and exploiting vulnerabilities in software, applications, or network devices.

Lateral Movement: Moving through the network using compromised credentials or exploiting weak configurations.

Data Exfiltration: Extracting sensitive data using covert channels, such as encrypted traffic or cloud storage services.

The choice of TTPs should reflect the adversary being emulated and the objectives of the operation.

Establish Rules of Engagement

The rules of engagement (ROE) are the guidelines that govern the red team operation. They define what actions are permitted, what systems or areas are off-limits, and how the operation will be conducted to ensure safety and compliance. Key elements of the ROE include:

Authorization: Ensure that the operation is authorized by senior management and that all relevant stakeholders are informed.

Safety Measures: Define measures to prevent unintended consequences, such as disrupting critical operations or causing data loss. This might include testing in isolated environments or using non-destructive methods.

Communication Protocols: Establish communication channels for the red team to report progress, escalate issues, or request assistance. This might include secure messaging apps, encrypted email, or dedicated communication platforms.

Post-Operation Cleanup: Define procedures for cleaning up any artifacts left by the red team, such as malware, scripts, or compromised credentials.

Assemble the Red Team

A successful red team operation requires a skilled and diverse team with expertise in various areas, such as network security, application security, physical security, and social engineering. Assemble a team with the right mix of skills and experience, and ensure that each member understands their role in the operation.

Executing Red Team Operations

Once the planning phase is complete, the red team can move on to executing the operation. The execution phase involves carrying out the attack, maintaining stealth, and gathering data for analysis. Here's how to execute a red team operation effectively:

Initial Access

The first step in the operation is to gain initial access to the target environment. Depending on the chosen TTPs, this might involve sending spear-phishing emails, exploiting a vulnerability, or gaining physical access to a facility. The red team should aim to achieve this access with minimal detection, avoiding actions that might trigger security alerts.

Establishing Persistence

Once initial access is gained, the red team must establish persistence to maintain control over the compromised systems. This could involve installing backdoors, creating hidden user accounts, or deploying malware that can be remotely controlled. The goal is to ensure that the red team can maintain access even if the initial point of compromise is discovered.

Privilege Escalation and Lateral Movement

With persistence established, the red team can begin escalating privileges to gain higher levels of access within the network. This might involve exploiting misconfigurations, stealing credentials, or using techniques like pass-the-hash. Once elevated privileges are obtained, the red team can move laterally through the network, exploring different systems and searching for high-value targets.

Achieving Objectives

The primary objectives of the red team operation are to achieve the goals defined during the planning phase. This could involve accessing sensitive data, disrupting services, or compromising critical systems. Throughout this process, the red team should remain stealthy, avoiding actions that might lead to detection or intervention by the blue team.

Data Exfiltration

If data exfiltration is one of the operation's objectives, the red team must find ways to extract data without triggering security alerts. This could involve encrypting the data, using steganography to hide it within other files, or leveraging legitimate channels like cloud storage or email. The red team should also consider how to evade data loss prevention (DLP) systems and other monitoring tools.

Maintain Stealth and Avoid Detection

Throughout the operation, the red team must prioritize stealth. This involves avoiding detection by security tools, blending in with normal network traffic, and using obfuscation techniques to hide their activities. If the red team is detected, they may attempt to cover their tracks by deleting logs, using anti-forensics techniques, or shifting tactics to evade further scrutiny.

Exit and Cleanup

Once the objectives are achieved, the red team should plan an exit strategy. This might involve removing any backdoors, malware, or other artifacts that could be discovered later. The team should also ensure that no evidence of their activities remains, such as cleaning up logs or deleting temporary files. The goal is to leave the environment in a state where the blue team has minimal evidence of the attack, making the operation as realistic as possible.

Post-Operation Analysis and Reporting

After the operation is complete, the red team should conduct a thorough analysis of the results. This involves reviewing the operation's effectiveness, assessing the organization's defenses, and providing recommendations for improvement. Here's how to conduct a post-operation analysis:

Review Key Metrics

Start by reviewing the key metrics established during the planning phase, such as detection times, response times, and the success of specific TTPs. Identify areas where the red team succeeded in achieving their objectives and areas where they encountered resistance.

Analyze Defensive Responses

Assess how well the blue team detected, responded to, and contained the simulated attack. This includes evaluating the effectiveness of security controls, monitoring tools, and incident response procedures. Identify any gaps or weaknesses that the red team was able to exploit.

Identify Strengths and Weaknesses

Based on the analysis, identify both strengths and weaknesses in the organization's defenses. Highlight any areas where the blue team performed well, such as early detection or effective containment, and any areas where improvements are needed.

Develop Recommendations

Provide actionable recommendations for improving the organization's defenses. This could include enhancing monitoring and detection capabilities, improving incident response procedures, or implementing additional security controls. The recommendations should be specific, achievable, and aligned with the organization's security goals.

Conduct a Debriefing

Hold a debriefing session with the red team, blue team, and other relevant stakeholders. Discuss the operation's results, share insights and lessons learned, and agree on the next steps for improving the organization's security posture. Use the debriefing as an opportunity to foster collaboration between the red and blue teams, helping them work together to strengthen the organization's defenses.

Document the Findings

Finally, document the findings of the red team operation in a detailed report. The report should include an overview of the operation, the objectives, the TTPs used, the results, and the recommendations for improvement. This report can serve as a valuable resource for the organization, helping to guide future security initiatives and inform decision-making.

Continuous Improvement

Red team operations should be part of a continuous cycle of testing, improvement, and reassessment. As the threat landscape evolves, organizations must regularly update their red team strategies, refine their TTPs, and enhance their defenses. By conducting regular red team operations and acting on the findings, organizations can stay ahead of emerging threats and build a more resilient security posture.

Conclusion

Red team operations are a powerful tool for testing and improving an organization's security defenses. By simulating real-world attacks and adopting the mindset of adversaries, red teams can identify weaknesses, challenge assumptions, and help organizations prepare for the most sophisticated threats. Through careful planning, execution, and analysis, red team operations can provide valuable insights that lead to stronger, more effective security measures.

In the next chapter, we will explore the importance of monitoring and logging in offensive security labs, focusing on how to capture and analyze data to gain a deeper understanding of security events and improve overall situational awareness.

Chapter 12: Monitoring and Logging for Offensive Labs

Monitoring and logging are critical components of any offensive security lab, providing the visibility needed to understand, analyze, and respond to security events. In an offensive security context, monitoring and logging serve multiple purposes: they help track the activities of both attackers and defenders, enable the detection of security incidents, and provide a detailed record for post-event analysis. Effective monitoring and logging allow you to capture the full spectrum of activities within your lab environment, from the initial reconnaissance phase of an attack to the final stages of data exfiltration. In this chapter, we will explore the tools and techniques for implementing robust monitoring and logging in your lab, as well as how to analyze and act on the data collected.

The Importance of Monitoring and Logging

Monitoring and logging are essential for several reasons:

Visibility: They provide a real-time view of activities within the network, helping you detect anomalies, unauthorized actions, and potential threats.

Incident Detection: Effective monitoring can help identify security incidents as they occur, enabling quicker response and mitigation.

Forensic Analysis: Logs provide a detailed record of events that can be analyzed after an incident to determine the cause, impact, and extent of the breach.

Compliance: Logging is often required for compliance with security standards and regulations, such as GDPR, HIPAA, or PCI-DSS.

Performance Evaluation: In an offensive security lab, monitoring and logging allow you to evaluate the performance of both defensive measures and attack simulations, providing insights into the effectiveness of your security strategies.

Key Components of Monitoring and Logging

To implement effective monitoring and logging, it's important to understand the key components involved:

Data Sources

Monitoring and logging begin with identifying the data sources that will provide the information you need. Common data sources include:

Network Traffic: Captured by network taps, span ports, or intrusion detection systems (IDS) to monitor communications between devices.

System Logs: Generated by operating systems, applications, and security tools, providing information on user activities, process execution, and system changes.

Security Appliances: Logs from firewalls, intrusion detection/prevention systems (IDS/IPS), and other security devices that provide insights into potential threats and blocked attacks.

Application Logs: Captured from web servers, databases, and other applications, providing details on access, errors, and user interactions.

Endpoint Logs: Logs from individual devices, such as laptops, servers, or IoT devices, capturing details on processes, file access, and network connections.

Audit Logs: Generated by security tools and monitoring systems, recording administrative actions, changes in configurations, and other critical activities.

Log Collection and Aggregation

Once the data sources are identified, the next step is to collect and aggregate logs from these sources into a centralized location for analysis. This can be achieved using tools like:

SIEM (Security Information and Event Management): SIEM systems collect, aggregate, and analyze log data from multiple sources, providing real-time insights and alerts based on predefined rules. Examples include Splunk, QRadar, and ELK Stack (Elasticsearch, Logstash, and Kibana).

Log Collectors: Tools like Fluentd, Logstash, and Graylog collect logs from various sources and normalize the data for analysis.

Syslog Servers: Syslog is a standard protocol used to send logs from devices and applications to a centralized server, where they can be stored and analyzed.

Real-Time Monitoring

Real-time monitoring involves actively observing network traffic, system activities, and log data to detect and respond to security incidents as they occur. Key tools and techniques include:

Network Monitoring: Tools like Wireshark, Zeek (formerly Bro), and SolarWinds monitor network traffic in real-time, capturing packets and analyzing them for signs of malicious activity.

Host-Based Monitoring: Tools like OSSEC and Wazuh monitor activities on individual hosts, such as file integrity changes, user logins, and process execution.

Intrusion Detection Systems (IDS): IDS tools like Snort, Suricata, and OpenWIPS-NG analyze network traffic for patterns that indicate potential attacks, triggering alerts when suspicious activities are detected.

Alerting and Notifications

Monitoring systems should be configured to generate alerts and notifications based on predefined rules and thresholds. These alerts can be sent via email, SMS, or integrated with incident management platforms like PagerDuty or ServiceNow. Alerts should be prioritized based on the severity of the detected activity, ensuring that critical incidents receive immediate attention.

Log Storage and Retention

Logs must be stored securely and retained for a specified period to ensure they are available for analysis, compliance audits, and forensic investigations. Consider the following when setting up log storage:

Retention Policies: Define retention policies based on regulatory requirements and organizational needs. For example, certain logs might need to be retained for seven years, while others can be deleted after 90 days.

Storage Solutions: Use centralized storage solutions that can handle large volumes of log data, such as distributed databases (e.g., Elasticsearch), cloud storage (e.g., AWS S3), or network-attached storage (NAS) devices.

Log Integrity: Ensure that logs are protected from tampering by implementing integrity checks, such as hashing, and by using secure storage methods, such as encryption.

Correlation and Analysis

Correlation and analysis involve linking related events across different data sources to identify patterns, detect anomalies, and uncover potential security incidents. This process is typically handled by SIEM systems, which use rules and machine learning algorithms to correlate events and generate insights.

Correlation Rules: Create correlation rules that link events from different sources, such as matching a failed login attempt with a subsequent suspicious network connection. These rules help identify complex attack patterns that might otherwise go unnoticed.

Anomaly Detection: Use anomaly detection algorithms to identify deviations from normal behavior, such as unexpected spikes in network traffic or unusual access patterns. These anomalies can indicate potential threats that require further investigation.

Dashboards and Reports: Use dashboards to visualize key metrics and trends, making it easier to spot patterns and assess the overall security posture. Regular reports can provide summaries of security events, system performance, and compliance status.

Implementing Monitoring and Logging in Your Offensive Lab

Setting up monitoring and logging in your offensive security lab requires careful planning and execution. Here's how to implement these capabilities effectively:

Identify Critical Assets

Start by identifying the critical assets in your lab that need to be monitored. These might include key servers, network devices, databases, and security tools. Understanding what needs to be monitored will help you determine the data sources and monitoring tools required.

Deploy Monitoring Tools

Deploy the appropriate monitoring tools across your lab environment. For network monitoring, consider using a combination of packet capture tools (e.g., Wireshark) and IDS systems (e.g., Snort). For host-based monitoring, deploy agents on critical servers and workstations to capture system logs and detect suspicious activities.

Configure Log Collection and Aggregation

Set up log collection and aggregation using a SIEM platform or log collector. Ensure that all relevant logs are being forwarded to the centralized log server and that they are being normalized for analysis. Configure the SIEM to generate alerts based on predefined rules, such as failed login attempts, privilege escalations, or large data transfers.

Establish Monitoring Dashboards

Create monitoring dashboards that provide a real-time view of activities within your lab environment. These dashboards should display key metrics such as network traffic, system performance, and security alerts. Consider using a customizable platform like Kibana to build dashboards that meet your specific needs.

Set Up Alerting and Incident Response

Configure alerting systems to notify you of potential security incidents. Ensure that alerts are prioritized based on their severity and that they are sent to the appropriate personnel for response. Integrate the alerting system with your incident response plan to ensure a coordinated and timely response to detected threats.

Regularly Review Logs and Alerts

Regularly review logs and alerts to identify potential issues and areas for improvement. Analyze any incidents that occur to determine their cause, impact, and how they were detected. Use this information to refine your monitoring and logging strategies, as well as to improve your overall security posture.

Test and Validate Monitoring Capabilities

Periodically test your monitoring and logging capabilities to ensure they are functioning as expected. This can involve conducting simulated attacks within your lab to see how well the monitoring tools detect and respond to threats. Use the results of these tests to make any necessary adjustments to your monitoring setup.

Analyzing and Acting on Collected Data

Once your monitoring and logging systems are in place, the next step is to analyze the data collected and take appropriate actions based on the insights gained. Here's how to approach this process:

Analyze Security Events

Start by analyzing the security events captured in your logs and monitoring tools. Look for patterns that indicate potential threats, such as repeated failed login attempts, unusual network connections, or unauthorized access to critical systems. Use correlation rules to link related events and identify complex attack scenarios.

Investigate Anomalies

Investigate any anomalies detected by your monitoring tools. This could involve reviewing logs in detail, conducting forensic analysis, or using threat intelligence to determine whether the anomaly is part of a larger attack. If an anomaly is found to be benign, update your monitoring rules to reduce false positives.

Respond to Incidents

When a security incident is detected, follow your incident response plan to contain and mitigate the threat. This might involve isolating compromised systems, blocking malicious traffic, or recovering documented for post-incident analysis.

Perform Post-Incident Analysis

After an incident has been contained and mitigated, conduct a thorough post-incident analysis to understand how the incident occurred, how it was detected, and how it was handled. Review logs, alerts, and any other data collected during the incident to identify the root cause and assess the effectiveness of your response.

During this analysis, consider the following questions:

How did the attacker gain initial access? Understanding the entry point can help you strengthen defenses against similar attacks in the future.

Were there any missed detection opportunities? Analyze whether any security events were overlooked or misinterpreted during the incident.

How effective was the incident response? Evaluate the speed and coordination of the response, as well as the adequacy of communication and decision-making.

What was the impact of the incident? Assess the damage caused by the incident, including data loss, operational disruption, or financial costs.

Update Security Measures

Based on the findings from your post-incident analysis, update your security measures to address any identified weaknesses. This could involve refining monitoring rules, enhancing detection capabilities, implementing additional security controls, or updating incident response procedures.

For example:

If the incident involved a phishing attack, you might implement more rigorous email filtering, enhance user training on phishing awareness, or adjust SIEM rules to detect suspicious email patterns.

If the attacker exploited a known vulnerability, ensure that all systems are fully patched and consider implementing a vulnerability management program to regularly identify and address potential weaknesses.

Enhance Threat Detection and Response

Use the insights gained from incidents and routine monitoring to continually improve your threat detection and response capabilities. This could involve:

Expanding Log Coverage: Ensure that all critical systems and applications are generating logs and that these logs are being collected and analyzed.

Implementing Advanced Detection Techniques: Consider adopting machine learning or behavioral analysis to detect more subtle or sophisticated threats that may evade traditional detection methods.

Automating Responses: Where possible, automate the response to common incidents, such as isolating infected machines or blocking known malicious IP addresses, to reduce response times and minimize the impact of incidents.

Regularly Review and Refine Monitoring Strategies

Monitoring and logging are not static processes; they should evolve as your organization grows and as new threats emerge. Regularly review your monitoring strategies, considering changes in the threat landscape, advancements in technology, and lessons learned from previous incidents.

During these reviews, ask yourself:

Are we capturing all relevant data? Ensure that your logging configuration captures the data needed to detect and analyze potential threats.

Are our alerting rules effective? Evaluate whether your alerts are appropriately prioritized and whether they generate actionable insights without causing alert fatigue.

Is our storage and retention policy adequate? Ensure that logs are stored securely and retained for a sufficient period to meet compliance requirements and support forensic investigations.

Conduct Regular Audits

Periodically conduct audits of your monitoring and logging systems to ensure they are functioning correctly and that all critical activities are being logged and monitored. These audits can help identify gaps in your coverage, misconfigurations, or other issues that could hinder your ability to detect and respond to security incidents.

Conclusion

Monitoring and logging are indispensable components of a robust offensive security lab. By capturing and analyzing data from across your environment, you gain the visibility needed to detect, respond to, and learn from security incidents. Effective monitoring and logging not only help you defend against current threats but also provide the insights necessary to continuously improve your security posture.

In the next chapter, we will explore how to conduct security assessments and penetration tests using the tools and techniques discussed throughout this book. These assessments will allow you to validate your defenses, identify vulnerabilities, and ensure that your lab environment is adequately prepared for real-world threats.

Chapter 13: Conducting Security Assessments and Penetration Tests

Security assessments and penetration tests are essential components of an organization's cybersecurity strategy. These activities help identify vulnerabilities, evaluate the effectiveness of security controls, and ensure that systems and networks are resilient against potential attacks. In an offensive security lab, conducting thorough security assessments and penetration tests is crucial for simulating real-world scenarios and understanding how attackers might exploit weaknesses in your defenses. In this chapter, we will explore the methodologies, tools, and best practices for conducting effective security assessments and penetration tests.

The Purpose of Security Assessments and Penetration Tests

Security assessments and penetration tests serve different but complementary purposes within an organization's security program:

Security Assessments: These are comprehensive evaluations of an organization's security posture, encompassing policies, procedures, technical controls, and overall risk management practices. Security assessments identify gaps in security controls, compliance issues, and areas for improvement.

Penetration Tests: Often referred to as "pen tests," these are focused, hands-on exercises that simulate real-world attacks against specific systems, applications, or networks. The goal is to identify and exploit vulnerabilities to assess how far an attacker could go within the environment. Penetration tests provide actionable insights into how to improve defenses and mitigate risks.

By conducting both security assessments and penetration tests, organizations can gain a holistic understanding of their security posture, from policy-level weaknesses to technical vulnerabilities that could be exploited by attackers.

Planning and Scoping Security Assessments and Penetration Tests

Before conducting a security assessment or penetration test, it's essential to clearly define the scope, objectives, and rules of engagement. Proper planning ensures that the assessment or test is aligned with the organization's goals and that all stakeholders are aware of the process and potential outcomes.

Define Objectives

Begin by defining the objectives of the security assessment or penetration test. Objectives should be specific, measurable, and aligned with the organization's overall security goals. Common objectives include:

Identifying Vulnerabilities: Discovering and prioritizing vulnerabilities in systems, networks, or applications that could be exploited by attackers.

Testing Security Controls: Evaluating the effectiveness of existing security controls, such as firewalls, intrusion detection systems (IDS), and encryption mechanisms.

Simulating Real-World Attacks: Mimicking the tactics, techniques, and procedures (TTPs) of known adversaries to assess the organization's ability to detect, respond to, and mitigate attacks.

Assessing Compliance: Ensuring that systems and processes comply with relevant security standards and regulations, such as PCI-DSS, HIPAA, or GDPR.

Determine Scope

The scope of the assessment or test defines what will be included and excluded from the evaluation. Scoping involves identifying the specific systems, applications, networks, and data that will be assessed. Key considerations include:

In-Scope Assets: Clearly define which assets are in scope, including IP ranges, domain names, servers, databases, and applications.

Out-of-Scope Assets: Identify any assets that are explicitly excluded from the assessment or test to avoid unintended disruptions or security breaches.

Testing Boundaries: Define the boundaries of the test, such as whether it will include internal networks, external networks, web applications, or wireless networks.

Establish Rules of Engagement

The rules of engagement (ROE) are the guidelines that govern how the assessment or test will be conducted. These rules ensure that the exercise is performed safely, ethically, and in accordance with organizational policies. Key elements of the ROE include:

Authorization: Obtain formal authorization from senior management to conduct the assessment or test. This ensures that all stakeholders are aware of the activity and that it is conducted with proper oversight.

Testing Hours: Define the time frame during which the assessment or test will take place. For example, testing might be restricted to non-business hours to minimize the impact on operations.

Communication Protocols: Establish communication channels for reporting progress, escalating issues, or pausing the test if necessary. This might include secure messaging apps, encrypted email, or dedicated communication platforms.

Incident Response Procedures: Define procedures for handling any incidents that arise during the assessment or test, such as unexpected system outages or detection by security monitoring tools.

Select the Testing Methodology

Choose a testing methodology that aligns with the objectives and scope of the assessment or test. Common methodologies include:

Black Box Testing: The tester has no prior knowledge of the target environment. This approach simulates an external attacker with no insider information, relying on publicly available information and reconnaissance to identify vulnerabilities.

White Box Testing: The tester has full knowledge of the target environment, including access to internal documentation, network diagrams, and source code. This approach is often used for thorough, in-depth assessments of specific systems or applications.

Gray Box Testing: The tester has limited knowledge of the target environment, such as partial access to internal information. This approach simulates an attacker with some insider knowledge, such as a disgruntled employee or a compromised vendor.

Conducting Security Assessments

Security assessments involve evaluating the organization's overall security posture, including policies, procedures, technical controls, and risk management practices. Here's how to conduct a comprehensive security assessment:

Review Security Policies and Procedures

Start by reviewing the organization's security policies and procedures to ensure they align with best practices and regulatory requirements. This includes policies related to data protection, access control, incident response, and vulnerability management. Identify any gaps or inconsistencies and provide recommendations for improvement.

Assess Technical Controls

Evaluate the effectiveness of the organization's technical controls, such as firewalls, IDS/IPS, encryption, and authentication mechanisms. This may involve reviewing configurations, testing security settings, and analyzing the implementation of security technologies.

Conduct Risk Assessments

Perform a risk assessment to identify and prioritize potential threats to the organization's assets. This involves evaluating the likelihood and impact of various threats, such as cyber attacks, data breaches, or insider threats. Use this information to recommend risk mitigation strategies.

Evaluate Compliance

Assess the organization's compliance with relevant security standards and regulations. This may involve reviewing audit logs, security documentation, and access controls to ensure they meet compliance requirements. Identify any areas of non-compliance and provide recommendations for remediation.

Report Findings

Document the findings of the security assessment in a detailed report. The report should include an overview of the assessment, identified risks and vulnerabilities, compliance gaps, and recommendations for improvement. Present the report to senior management and other stakeholders to inform decision-making and guide future security initiatives.

Conducting Penetration Tests

Penetration tests involve simulating real-world attacks against specific systems, applications, or networks to identify and exploit vulnerabilities. Here's how to conduct an effective penetration test:

Reconnaissance and Information Gathering

The first step in a penetration test is to gather information about the target environment. This may involve:

Passive Reconnaissance: Collecting publicly available information, such as domain names, IP addresses, email addresses, and organizational details, without interacting directly with the target systems.

Active Reconnaissance: Actively probing the target environment using tools like Nmap to identify open ports, running services, and network configurations.

Vulnerability Scanning

Use automated vulnerability scanning tools to identify potential weaknesses in the target systems. Common tools include:

Nessus: A widely-used vulnerability scanner that identifies known vulnerabilities, misconfigurations, and compliance issues.

OpenVAS: An open-source vulnerability scanner that provides comprehensive scanning capabilities for various systems and applications.

Burp Suite: A web vulnerability scanner that identifies issues like SQL injection, cross-site scripting (XSS), and other web application vulnerabilities.

Exploitation

After identifying vulnerabilities, the next step is to exploit them to gain access to the target systems. This involves using penetration testing frameworks like Metasploit or custom exploits to achieve the following objectives:

Gaining Access: Exploiting vulnerabilities to gain unauthorized access to systems or applications.

Privilege Escalation: Elevating privileges to gain administrative or root access on the target systems.

Lateral Movement: Moving laterally within the network to access additional systems, applications, or data.

Post-Exploitation

Once access is gained, the focus shifts to maintaining access, gathering information, and achieving the test's objectives. Post-exploitation activities may include:

Data Exfiltration: Extracting sensitive data from the target systems, such as customer records, financial information, or intellectual property.

Persistence: Installing backdoors or creating hidden user accounts to maintain access over time.

Covering Tracks: Deleting logs, disabling security tools, or using anti-forensic techniques to avoid detection.

Reporting and Remediation

After the penetration test is complete, document the findings in a detailed report. The report should include:

Executive Summary: A high-level overview of the test's objectives, scope, and key findings, written for non-technical stakeholders.

Detailed Findings: A technical breakdown of the vulnerabilities identified, how they were exploited, and the potential impact on the organization.

Recommendations: Actionable recommendations for remediating the identified vulnerabilities and strengthening the organization's defenses.

Present the report to the relevant stakeholders and work with the organization's IT and security teams to implement the recommended remediation measures.

Post-Assessment and Continuous Improvement

After completing a security assessment or penetration test, it's important to follow up on the findings and take steps to continuously improve the organization's security posture. Here's how to approach this:

Implement Remediation Measures

Work with the organization's IT and security teams to implement the remediation measures recommended in the assessment or test report. This may involve patching vulnerabilities, reconfiguring security controls, or updating policies and procedures.

Conduct Follow-Up Assessments

After implementing remediation measures, conduct follow-up assessments or tests to verify that the vulnerabilities have been effectively addressed. This ensures that the organization's security posture has improved and that no new vulnerabilities have been introduced.

Refine Security Strategies

Use the insights gained from the assessment or test to refine the organization's overall security strategies. This may involve updating risk management practices, enhancing monitoring and detection capabilities, or investing in new security technologies.

Foster a Culture of Continuous Improvement

Encourage a culture of continuous improvement within the organization, where security assessments and penetration tests are conducted regularly, and lessons learned are used to strengthen defenses. This proactive approach helps the organization stay ahead of emerging threats and maintain a strong security posture over time.

Conclusion

Conducting security assessments and penetration tests is a critical part of maintaining a robust security posture in any organization. These activities provide valuable insights into vulnerabilities, the effectiveness of security controls, and the organization's ability to defend against real-world attacks. By following a structured approach to planning, executing, and analyzing these tests, organizations can identify weaknesses, implement effective remediation measures, and continuously improve their defenses.

In the next chapter, we will explore training and skill development for cyber teams, focusing on how to use your offensive security lab as a platform for hands-on learning and professional growth.

Chapter 14: Training and Skill Development for Cyber Teams

Training and skill development are critical components of any successful cybersecurity program. The rapidly evolving threat landscape requires that cyber teams continuously update their knowledge and skills to stay ahead of adversaries. An offensive security lab offers an ideal environment for hands-on training, allowing team members to practice their skills in a controlled, realistic setting. In this chapter, we will explore strategies for using your offensive security lab to enhance the training and professional development of your cyber teams. We will also discuss various training methodologies, the importance of continuous learning, and how to measure the effectiveness of your training programs.

The Importance of Hands-On Training

While theoretical knowledge is essential, hands-on training is crucial for developing practical skills that cyber professionals can apply in real-world situations. An offensive security lab provides a safe environment where team members can:

Practice Offensive Techniques: Team members can hone their skills in areas such as penetration testing, red teaming, and exploit development without the risk of disrupting live systems.

Test Defensive Strategies: Blue teams can practice detecting, responding to, and mitigating attacks, improving their ability to protect the organization from real threats.

Understand Adversary Tactics: By simulating attacks, team members gain a deeper understanding of the tactics, techniques, and procedures (TTPs) used by adversaries, enabling them to anticipate and defend against similar attacks in the real world.

Collaborate and Learn Together: The lab environment fosters collaboration and knowledge sharing among team members, helping to build a more cohesive and capable security team.

Developing a Training Program

A well-structured training program is essential for ensuring that your cyber teams develop the skills they need to protect the organization effectively. Here's how to design and implement a comprehensive training program using your offensive security lab:

Assess Training Needs

Start by assessing the current skill levels of your team members and identifying any gaps in their knowledge or experience. Consider factors such as:

Technical Skills: Evaluate the team's proficiency in areas such as network security, web application security, incident response, and threat hunting.

Soft Skills: Assess the team's abilities in areas such as communication, collaboration, and problem-solving, which are essential for effective teamwork.

Certifications and Qualifications: Review any relevant certifications or qualifications that team members may need to obtain or renew, such as Certified Ethical Hacker (CEH), Offensive Security Certified Professional (OSCP), or Certified Information Systems Security Professional (CISSP).

Based on this assessment, identify the specific skills and knowledge areas that need to be developed and prioritize them according to the organization's security goals.

Set Training Objectives

Define clear, measurable objectives for the training program. These objectives should be aligned with the organization's security strategy and the individual career goals of team members. Common training objectives include:

Improving Penetration Testing Skills: Enhancing the team's ability to identify and exploit vulnerabilities in systems and applications.

Enhancing Incident Response Capabilities: Strengthening the team's ability to detect, respond to, and recover from security incidents.

Developing Threat Hunting Skills: Training team members to proactively search for signs of compromise and emerging threats within the network.

Building Red Team Expertise: Preparing team members to conduct red team operations that simulate advanced adversary tactics.

Design Training Scenarios

Use your offensive security lab to create realistic training scenarios that reflect the types of threats and challenges the organization is likely to face. These scenarios should be tailored to the skill levels and learning objectives of the participants. Examples of training scenarios include:

Phishing Simulation: Simulate a phishing attack to test the team's ability to recognize, report, and respond to social engineering threats.

Network Intrusion Exercise: Create a scenario where attackers attempt to gain access to the network, and the team must detect and mitigate the intrusion.

Web Application Exploitation: Develop a scenario that involves exploiting vulnerabilities in a web application, such as SQL injection or cross-site scripting (XSS).

Incident Response Drill: Conduct a simulated security incident, such as a ransomware attack, and have the team practice their response procedures, including containment, eradication, and recovery.

Implement Blended Learning

A blended learning approach combines hands-on exercises with theoretical instruction, providing a well-rounded training experience. Components of a blended learning program might include:

Instructor-Led Training (ILT): Traditional classroom-style training sessions led by experienced instructors, covering topics such as security fundamentals, compliance requirements, and best practices.

Online Learning Modules: Self-paced online courses that allow team members to study specific topics in depth, such as malware analysis, cryptography, or cloud security.

Lab-Based Exercises: Practical exercises conducted in the offensive security lab, where team members apply what they have learned in realistic scenarios.

Workshops and Seminars: Interactive sessions where team members can discuss challenges, share insights, and collaborate on solving complex security problems.

Encourage Continuous Learning

Cybersecurity is a rapidly evolving field, and continuous learning is essential for staying ahead of new threats and technologies. Encourage team members to pursue ongoing education and professional development by:

Providing Access to Resources: Give team members access to a wide range of learning resources, such as books, online courses, webinars, and conferences.

Offering Certification Support: Support team members in obtaining relevant certifications by covering exam fees, providing study materials, and offering time off for exam preparation.

Promoting Knowledge Sharing: Create opportunities for team members to share their knowledge and experiences with each other, such as through internal training sessions, lunch-and-learn events, or discussion groups.

Encouraging Participation in CTFs: Capture the Flag (CTF) competitions are a fun and challenging way for team members to practice their skills and learn new techniques. Encourage participation in CTF events, either individually or as a team.

Measuring Training Effectiveness

To ensure that your training program is effective, it's important to measure the outcomes and make adjustments as needed. Here's how to evaluate the effectiveness of your training program:

Assess Skill Improvement

Measure the improvement in team members' skills over time by conducting regular assessments and comparing the results to baseline measurements taken before the training began. This can include practical exercises, quizzes, or performance reviews.

Monitor Performance in Real-World Scenarios

Evaluate how well team members apply their training in real-world situations, such as during security incidents, penetration tests, or red team operations. Look for improvements in areas such as detection times, response effectiveness, and problem-solving abilities.

Gather Feedback from Participants

Collect feedback from team members about the training program, including what they found valuable, what challenges they encountered, and what areas they would like to explore further. Use this feedback to refine the training program and address any gaps or weaknesses.

Track Certification and Career Progression

Monitor the progress of team members in obtaining relevant certifications and advancing their careers within the organization. This can provide a tangible measure of the success of the training program and demonstrate its value to senior management.

Evaluate Organizational Impact

Assess the overall impact of the training program on the organization's security posture. This can include metrics such as the number of security incidents detected, the speed and effectiveness of incident response, and improvements in compliance with security standards and regulations.

Building a Culture of Continuous Improvement

To maximize the effectiveness of your training program, it's important to foster a culture of continuous improvement within your cyber teams. This involves creating an environment where learning and development are prioritized, and where team members are encouraged to take ownership of their growth. Here's how to build this culture:

Lead by Example

Encourage senior leaders and managers to participate in training and skill development activities, demonstrating their commitment to continuous improvement. When leaders prioritize learning, it sets a positive example for the entire team.

Recognize and Reward Achievement

Recognize and reward team members who demonstrate a commitment to learning and professional development. This can include formal recognition, such as awards or bonuses, as well as informal recognition, such as praise from peers and managers.

Provide Opportunities for Growth

Offer team members opportunities to take on new challenges and expand their skill sets, such as by leading projects, participating in cross-functional teams, or mentoring junior staff. These opportunities help team members apply what they have learned and continue to grow professionally.

Encourage Experimentation and Innovation

Create a safe environment where team members can experiment with new techniques, tools, and approaches without fear of failure. Encourage innovation by supporting creative problem-solving and rewarding successful initiatives.

Promote a Learning Mindset

Cultivate a mindset of curiosity and continuous learning within the team. Encourage team members to stay informed about the latest developments in cybersecurity, to ask questions, and to seek out new knowledge and skills.

Conclusion

Training and skill development are essential for building a capable and resilient cybersecurity team. By leveraging your offensive security lab as a platform for hands-on learning, you can provide your team members with the practical experience they need to defend against real-world threats. A well-designed training program, combined with a culture of continuous improvement, ensures that your cyber teams are always ready to meet the challenges of an ever-evolving threat landscape.

In the next chapter, we will discuss how to maintain and evolve your offensive security lab to ensure that it remains a valuable resource for training, testing, and research as your organization's needs grow and change.

Chapter 15: Maintaining and Evolving the Security Lab

An offensive security lab is not a static entity; it must evolve to keep pace with emerging threats, new technologies, and the growing needs of your organization. Proper maintenance and continual evolution of the lab are essential to ensure that it remains an effective tool for security testing, training, and research. In this final chapter, we will explore strategies for maintaining your security lab, adapting to new challenges, and planning for future growth. We will also discuss how to leverage the lab as a dynamic resource that contributes to the overall security posture of your organization.

The Importance of Continuous Maintenance

Regular maintenance of your offensive security lab is crucial to ensure that it functions correctly and remains aligned with the organization's security goals. Maintenance activities include updating software, managing hardware resources, and refining configurations. Here's why continuous maintenance is important:

Ensuring Reliability: Regular maintenance helps prevent technical issues, such as system crashes or network failures, that could disrupt testing or training activities.

Staying Current with Threats: The threat landscape is constantly changing. By regularly updating the tools and systems in your lab, you can simulate the latest threats and test your defenses against current attack techniques.

Compliance and Security: Keeping your lab environment up to date with the latest security patches and configurations helps protect it from vulnerabilities that could be exploited by attackers during testing.

Maximizing Resource Efficiency: Maintenance helps ensure that your lab's resources—such as processing power, storage, and network bandwidth—are used efficiently and are available when needed for testing and training.

Routine Maintenance Activities

To keep your lab environment in top shape, establish a routine maintenance schedule that covers the following activities:

Software and Tool Updates

Regularly update all software and tools used in the lab, including operating systems, security tools, and virtualization platforms. Ensure that all updates are tested in a controlled environment before deployment to avoid compatibility issues or disruptions. Key updates include:

Operating Systems: Apply security patches and updates to all operating systems used in your lab environment, including virtual machines and physical hosts.

Security Tools: Update security tools like vulnerability scanners, IDS/IPS systems, and SIEM platforms to ensure they are equipped to detect the latest threats.

Exploitation Frameworks: Update penetration testing frameworks, such as Metasploit, to access the latest exploits and payloads.

Custom Scripts and Code: Review and update any custom scripts, tools, or code used in your lab to ensure they remain functional and secure.

Hardware Maintenance

Monitor the health and performance of your lab's hardware resources, including servers, networking equipment, and storage devices. Key maintenance tasks include:

Hardware Diagnostics: Run regular diagnostics on servers, storage devices, and networking equipment to identify any potential hardware issues.

Resource Allocation: Ensure that resources like CPU, memory, and storage are allocated efficiently across virtual machines and applications to prevent bottlenecks and ensure optimal performance.

Hardware Upgrades: Plan for hardware upgrades as needed to support new testing scenarios, additional users, or increased workloads. This might include adding more RAM, upgrading processors, or expanding storage capacity.

Backup and Disaster Recovery

Implement a robust backup and disaster recovery plan for your lab environment to protect against data loss and ensure continuity of operations. Key components include:

Regular Backups: Schedule regular backups of critical systems, configurations, and data. Store backups in a secure, off-site location or use cloud-based backup services.

Disaster Recovery Testing: Periodically test your disaster recovery plan to ensure that backups can be restored quickly and that the lab environment can be brought back online in the event of a failure.

Network and Security Configurations

Review and update network and security configurations to ensure they align with current best practices and organizational requirements. Key tasks include:

Firewall and IDS/IPS Rules: Review and update firewall and IDS/IPS rules to ensure they are effective in blocking unauthorized traffic and detecting potential threats.

Access Controls: Verify that access controls are properly configured to restrict access to sensitive systems and data within the lab environment. Implement multi-factor authentication (MFA) and role-based access controls (RBAC) where appropriate.

Network Segmentation: Ensure that network segmentation is correctly configured to isolate different testing environments and prevent unauthorized access between segments.

Documentation and Inventory Management

Maintain up-to-date documentation and inventory records for all systems, tools, and configurations in your lab environment. This documentation is essential for troubleshooting, audits, and future planning. Key elements include:

System Configurations: Document the configurations of all systems and applications, including IP addresses, firewall rules, and network topologies.

Inventory Management: Keep an accurate inventory of all hardware and software assets in your lab, including licenses, version numbers, and expiration dates.

Change Logs: Maintain a change log that records all updates, modifications, and configuration changes made to the lab environment. This log is essential for tracking the history of the environment and understanding the impact of changes.

Evolving the Lab to Meet New Challenges

As your organization grows and the threat landscape evolves, your security lab must adapt to meet new challenges. Evolving the lab involves expanding its capabilities, integrating new technologies, and staying ahead of emerging threats. Here's how to approach this evolution:

Expand Testing Capabilities

To keep pace with the growing complexity of modern attacks, consider expanding your lab's testing capabilities. This might involve:

Cloud Security Testing: As organizations increasingly adopt cloud services, it's essential to test the security of cloud-based environments. Expand your lab to include cloud platforms like AWS, Azure, and Google Cloud, and test for vulnerabilities specific to these environments.

Mobile Security Testing: With the proliferation of mobile devices, include mobile security testing in your lab's capabilities. This involves testing mobile applications, operating systems, and the security of mobile communications.

IoT Security Testing: As the Internet of Things (IoT) continues to grow, add IoT devices to your lab environment and test for vulnerabilities in IoT ecosystems. This includes testing the security of IoT devices, communication protocols, and associated applications.

Integrate Emerging Technologies

Stay ahead of the curve by integrating emerging technologies into your lab environment. This includes:

Artificial Intelligence and Machine Learning: Integrate AI and machine learning tools to enhance threat detection, automate analysis, and develop more sophisticated attack simulations.

Blockchain and Cryptography: As blockchain technology becomes more prevalent, include blockchain networks and smart contracts in your testing scenarios. Test for vulnerabilities in blockchain implementations and cryptographic protocols.

Software-Defined Networking (SDN) and Network Function Virtualization (NFV): Incorporate SDN and NFV technologies into your lab to test the security of virtualized network infrastructures and dynamic network configurations.

Simulate Advanced Threats

Continuously update your lab's threat simulation capabilities to reflect the latest adversary tactics, techniques, and procedures (TTPs). This might involve:

Threat Intelligence Integration: Integrate real-time threat intelligence feeds into your lab to simulate the latest threats and test your defenses against current attack vectors.

Adversary Emulation: Use tools like MITRE ATT&CK to emulate the behavior of specific adversary groups, simulating their attack techniques and testing your organization's ability to defend against them.

Advanced Persistent Threat (APT) Simulations: Develop scenarios that mimic APTs, focusing on long-term, stealthy attacks that target critical assets within the organization.

Plan for Future Growth

As your organization and its security needs evolve, plan for the future growth of your lab environment. This includes:

Scalability: Ensure that your lab environment is scalable, with the ability to accommodate more users, systems, and testing scenarios as needed. This might involve adding additional servers, storage, and networking resources.

Collaboration and Sharing: Consider expanding your lab to support collaboration with other teams, departments, or external partners. This might involve setting up shared environments, secure access controls, and collaborative tools.

Budgeting and Resource Allocation: Plan for the financial and resource needs of your lab's growth. This includes budgeting for hardware and software upgrades, licensing costs, and ongoing maintenance.

Stay Informed and Adapt

The cybersecurity landscape is constantly changing, with new threats, technologies, and best practices emerging regularly. To keep your lab relevant and effective:

Continuous Learning: Encourage continuous learning within your team to stay informed about the latest developments in cybersecurity. This includes attending conferences, participating in webinars, and reading industry publications.

Community Engagement: Engage with the broader cybersecurity community to share knowledge, collaborate on research, and learn from the experiences of others. This might involve participating in open-source projects, contributing to forums, or joining industry groups.

Regular Reviews and Audits: Conduct regular reviews and audits of your lab environment to assess its effectiveness and identify areas for improvement. Use these reviews to inform future planning and evolution.

Leveraging the Lab as a Strategic Asset

As your lab evolves, it can become a strategic asset that contributes to the overall security posture of your organization. Here's how to leverage your lab as a dynamic resource:

Enhance Security Testing and Assurance

Use your lab to conduct regular security testing and assurance activities, such as penetration tests, vulnerability assessments, and red team exercises. These activities help validate the effectiveness of your security controls and ensure that your defenses are capable of withstanding real-world attacks.

Support Incident Response and Threat Hunting

Leverage your lab as a platform for incident response and threat hunting. This includes using the lab to simulate attacks, analyze malware, and develop detection and response strategies. The lab can also serve as a sandbox environment for analyzing and mitigating threats without risking live systems.

Facilitate Research and Development

Use your lab to conduct research and development (R&D) activities, such as exploring new security technologies, developing custom tools, and testing innovative defense strategies. The lab provides a safe and controlled environment for experimentation and innovation.

Provide Training and Skill Development

Continue to use your lab as a training platform for developing the skills of your cyber teams. Regularly update training scenarios to reflect the latest threats and challenges, and provide opportunities for hands-on learning and professional growth.

Contribute to Organizational Resilience

By continuously evolving and leveraging your lab, you contribute to the overall resilience of your organization. The insights gained from lab activities help strengthen your defenses, improve your incident response capabilities, and prepare your organization for future challenges.

Conclusion

Maintaining and evolving your offensive security lab is essential for ensuring that it remains a valuable resource for security testing, training, and research. By implementing regular maintenance activities, expanding your lab's capabilities, and planning for future growth, you can keep your lab aligned with the evolving needs of your organization and the changing threat landscape. As a dynamic and strategic asset, your lab plays a crucial role in enhancing your organization's security posture and preparing it to defend against the most sophisticated and persistent threats.

This concludes the final chapter of your book. The content provided outlines a comprehensive approach to building, maintaining, and leveraging an offensive security lab as a critical resource for any organization's cybersecurity efforts. If you have any further requests, such as additional content, revisions, or any specific focus areas, feel free to ask!

Made in the USA
Columbia, SC
12 September 2024

d50c9da9-d980-4a29-a3f1-70ec3e88cc2aR01